Management of Libraries & Information Centers

Management of Libraries and Information Centers

Dr. P. Balasubramanian
M.A., M.B.A., M.C.A., M.L.I.Sc., M.Phil., PGDPR, Ph.D.
University Librarian & Head
Department of Library & Information Science
Manonmaiam Sundaranar University
Tirunelveli 627012
Tamil Nadu
India

Ess Ess Publications
New Delhi

Management of Libraries & Information Centers

ISBN : 978-93-87698-30-7
Price : Rs. 900/-

First Published 2021

Published by:
Ess Ess Publications
4831/24, Ansari Road,
Darya Ganj,
New Delhi-110 002.
INDIA
Phones: 23260807, 41563444
Fax: 41563334
E-mail: info@essessreference.com
www.essessreference.com

Cover Design by *Patch Creative Unit*

Printed and bound in India

Dedicated to

MY BELOVED PARENTS

Contents

Preface

As a part of the curriculum and in order to gain practical knowledge in the field of Library Management **"Management of Libraries & Information Centers"** The Basic Objective behind writing this book is to get knowledge from different tools of Libraries

In this book we have included various concept, effects and implication regarding Library Management. Subject matter of this report has been elaborated with simple words. Table, figure has been given to facilitate understanding.

I gave my complete effort to make it valuable, useful and enrich it with my views so that it give complete sense and benefit to readers. I hope who goes through it will find it interesting and worth reading. All constructive feedback is cordially invited.

Suggestion to new ideas for further improvement of this book shall be greatly appreciated and acknowledged.

I acknowledge my heartfelt gratitude to Prof. Dr. A. Rangaswamy, for invaluable advice and suggestions.

Finally, I would like to acknowledge the pleasure of working with publishing team of ESS ESS Publications, New Delhi.

— **Dr. P. Balasubramanian**

Acknowledgements

The author feels extremely indebted to Dr. K. Pitchumani, Hon'ble Vice-Chancellor, Manonmaniam Sundaranar University, Tirunelveli. We also thank Dr. S. Santhosh Baboo, Registrar, Manonmaniam Sundaranar University, Tirunelveli and all the teaching and non-teaching staff members of the M.S. University, for giving us constant encouragement for writing this book.

We would be a benefit killer if we do not acknowledge the services of Ess Ess Publications, New Delhi for their efforts in bringing out this book in a record time. Suggestions for further improvement of the book are most welcome.

— Dr. P. Balasubramanian

1

Basics of Management

LEARNING OBJECTIVES

After reading this unit, you will be able to

- Describe the term management as applied to libraries and information center;
- Identify the fundamental components of management, planning, organizing, staffing, directing and control;
- Demonstrate management skill in libraries and information centers.
- Discuss the levels of management.
- To understand the Management Information System (MIS).

1.1. INTRODUCTION

A library is a gathering of information, assets, and services, and the way of structure in which it was stored; it is gathered mainly for the purpose of usage and retains by public, an organization, or a single person. In the customary way, a library is a collection of books in one place. It can mean the gathering itself, the structure or area that holds such a collection, or both. The word "library" itself has another meaning: "a group of useful resource for public use." This term mainly used in departments such as technology (computer science), analytical and environmental science. It is also used by publishers in categorizing series of books in same genre, e.g. The Anglo-Catholic Religion Library.

Public and collections for scholar and services which may intend for the usage of people who didn't want to or could not afford to buy an expensive and vast collection by themselves, who need resource no person can logically be expected to have, or who need special support with their research. Also in addition to distributing resources, libraries also provide the assistance of individuals who are professionals at gathering and organizing information and at construing information needs. Library is a place provides silent environment for studying.

Modern libraries are the main source and access points for photocopy, audio and video resources in various formats, as well as maps, documents, microform, CDs, cassettes, videotapes, DVDS, video game, audio books and several other automated resources. They always give public services to access to their Internet service and other electronic resources. Nowadays Modern libraries are being labeled mainly as places to get open access to information in any formats and from any sources. Their service will reach beyond the walls of a building, by making resources accessible by electronic means, and by providing the support of librarians in finding and researching large quantity of information with a help of digitalization.

Monitoring a composite organization in order to accomplish certain goals resulted in altering the course of the concept of management. Management means every person who is concerned with managing an organization. It is not a single man's job, a sum of organized events done by a group of people. It also includes decision making in an organization at various levels of situation for getting things done. It is both science as well as an art, because the basic principles of management are same everywhere but the way of doing is differ.

"Management is a different process which includes of preparation, establishing, initiating and monitoring to define and achieve the objectives by using people and resources."

— *G.R. Terry*

"Management is just the process of making decisions and control over the action of individuals for the direct resolve of achieving pre-determined goals."

— *Stanley Vance*

"Management is a skill, getting things finished through and with the individuals in properly organized groups."

— *Harold Koontz*

Fig. 1

Meaning and Scope

It is very hard to define management exactly the way it is. There is no general term for defining management. It involves both acquirement and presentation of knowledge. However, it is a mixture of both an art and science. The scientific come lies in decision-making, scheduling and in the suitable exploit of technology. The artistic come to management can be established in the tasks of communicating, leadership and goal-setting. Some commonly used definitions of management are given below:

- Management is an art or process of getting things done through the efforts of other individuals.
- Management is an art of generating and maintaining of an inside environment of an organization where individuals, working together in group, can perform efficiently and effectively towards the achievement of determined goals.
- Management is the method of setting and achieving goals through the execution of five vital management functions that utilize man power, financial and material resources.
- Management is a technique or an action that brings together many different resources like individuals, constituents, techniques and technologies to achieve a single task or multiple tasks.
- Since it is a separate field of study, is also the frame of organized information which underlies the art of management.

The definitions and a review of management literature would uncover the following characteristics of management.

- Managing is an act or process;
- It make things happen;
- It is determined which means the achievement of an organization's goals and objectives is the significant purpose;
- It is supported and not replaced through the computer; and
- It is intangible.
- It uses accessible resources economically to increase outputs;
- The organization's objectives are achieved through,

with single person or through the attempts of a group;

- Management indicates by certain skills, knowledge and practices to increase effectiveness;

Concept of Management

Some of the common definition of management given by famous writers and researchers are:

According to Harold Koontz and Heinz Weihrich, Management is a process of planning and maintaining an environment in which individuals, working together in groups, efficiently accomplish determined goals.

According to Robert L. Trewelly and M. Gene Newport, Management is defined as the process of planning, organizing, motivating and directing an organization's operations in order to achieve co-ordination among workers and resources which is essential in the effective and efficient accomplishment of objectives.

According to Kreitner, "Management is the process of working with and through others to effectively achieve organizational objectives by efficiently using limited resources in the changing environment.

So Management can be defined as a process of getting things done with the aim of achieving goals effectively and efficiently. Some important terms in this definition are:

Process : Process is the main function or activity which performed by management in the process of get things done. These functions are planning, organizing, recruitment, leading and monitoring.

Effectiveness : Effectiveness is mainly certain about with the end result. It basically means completing the given task. Therefore doing the right task, completing activities and achieving goals are concerned by effectiveness in management.

Efficient : Efficiency means making the right amount of efforts for the task correctly and in more cost efficient way. Management is concerned with the efficient use of the resources which ultimately reduce costs and lead to higher profits.

It is important for management to accomplish their objectives (effectiveness) with minimum resources i.e., as efficiently as possible while maintaining a balance between effectiveness and efficiency.

Nature of Management

The management is one of the oldest practices in human civilization. As a fact, most of the evolution of mankind past few centuries may be credited to the effective resources management. The irrigation method, the public resources, the creation of various memorials like Taj Mahal, and the Egyptian Pyramids of the bygone era liberally validate the practice of management in the historic period. Likewise, the ancient civilizations of Mesopotamia, Greece, Rome and Indus-valley displayed the significant practices of management of those periods. However, the study of management in a systematic way as a distinct body of knowledge is only of recent origin.

As a result, over the past few decades, the backdrop of industrial activity had undertaken a major change. An individual's mission for new ways of doing things, joined with his resourcefulness in adopting the scientific and technological developments in the production of goods and services resulted in:

- Increase in production during the expectation of demand;
- Arrival of organization in corporate form will provide large amount production;
- Major developments in the transport and communication facilities;
- More competition in markets;

- Creating more effective relationship between employer – employee; and
- A drastic change in the objectives and prospects of the various investors of business.

Administration

A systematic process of directing the management of a business organization is known as administration, in educational institution like school or college, government office or any non-profit organization. The major role of administration is the construction of a plan, policies, and procedures, fixing goals and objectives, implementing rules and regulations, etc.

Administration puts down the fundamental basis of an organization, within which management of the functions of organization.

The administration's nature is organizational. It is a larger term as it includes organizing, estimating, planning and decision-making functions at the highest level of an organization. Administration represents the highest level of the management pyramid of an organization. These authorities of top level are the either proprietors or partners in business, who invest their capital in the starting of business. They will be paid return in the form of profits or as a dividend.

Management Attributes

Management in general term defined as an action of handling individuals and their job, for achieving the objective of the organization by using its resources. It produces an environment under which the subordinates and their manager can work together for the achievement of group objective. It is in order to run the complete system of the organization a group of people will use their skills and talent. It is an action, a function, a process, a discipline and much more.

Planning, organizing, leading, motivating, controlling, coordination and decision making are the majorly performed activities by the management. It will bring together the major factors of the organization, which is commonly known as 5M's of an organization Men, Material, Machines, Methods, and Money. This activity mainly concentrates on the result, which focuses on achieving the anticipated output.

Difference Between Administration and Management

Basis for Comparison	*Management*	*Administration*
Meaning	A way of managing people and organizing the objectives of a business is called as the Management.	The process of managing an organization by a group of people is known as the Administration.
Authority	Lower Level and Middle	Top level
Role	Executive	Decisive
Concerned with	Policy Implementation	Policy Formulation
Area of operation	It works under administration.	It has full control over the activities of the organization.
Applicable to	Profit making organizations, i.e. business organizations.	Government offices, military, clubs, business enterprises, hospitals, religious and educational organizations.
Decides	Who should do the work? And How the work has to be done?	What should be done? And When it should be done?
Work	Putting plans and policies into actions.	Formulation of plans, framing policies and setting objectives
Focus on	Managing work	Making best possible allocation of limited resources.

Key person	Manager	Administrator
Represents	Employees, who work for remuneration	Owners, who get a return on the capital invested by them.
Function	Executive and Governing	Legislative and Determinative

Key Differences between Management and Administration

The major differences between management and administration are given below:

1. Management is a methodical way of handling people and things within the organization. The administration is defined as an action of controlling the entire organization by a group of people.
2. Management is a part of business and functional level, whereas Administration is an activity of high-level.
3. While management concentrates on policy employment, policy creation is done by the administration.
4. Role of administration includes rules and healthy structure. On the other hand, role of management are decision-making and directing.
5. All the important decisions of the organization are taken by administration, while management makes decisions within the limitations fixed by the administration.
6. Management is known as, a cluster of individuals who are the workers of an organization. However, the owners of the organization are represents by administration.
7. Profit making organization like business enterprises are the general stage for Management. On the other hand, the Administration is a place to be found in government and military force, clubs, medical

facilities, establishments based on religious and all the enterprises with zero profits.

8. Management is all about strategies and activities, but the administration is concerned with creating policies and setting a goal for the organization.
9. Management has an administrative part in the organization. Unlike administration, this will take part in vital position in nature.
10. The manager is the major decision making authority in the management of the organization, whereas administrator is the major decision making authority for the administration of the organization.
11. Management concentrates on handling people and their work. On the other hand, administration concentrates on making the best way of utilization of the organization's resources.

Functions of Management

Management has been defined as a communal process in which includes concern for economical and effective planning & guidelines for process of an organization in the serenity of given purposes. It contains of various elements and activities in its dynamic process. These processes are different from operational functions like marketing, finance, purchase etc. Rather these processes are equal to all mangers irrespective of his level or status.

Many professionals have categorized management functions. According to authors George & Jerry, "There are five fundamental functions of management i.e. planning, organizing, staffing, directing and controlling".

Henry Fayol, said that "To manage is to prediction and strategy, to organize, to command, & to control". Whereas Luther Gullick has given a short term 'POSDCORB' where P is for Planning, O for Organizing, S for Staffing, D for Directing, Co for Co-ordination, R for reporting & B for Budgeting. But the most commonly known functions of management are given by KOONTZ and O'DONNEL i.e. Planning, Organizing, Staffing, Directing and Controlling.

For academic purposes, it may be suitable to separate the function of management but practically these functions are cannot be separated in nature i.e. they are joined at the hip. Each function combines with the each & other which affect the performance of others.

Planning

It is the fundamental role of management. It deals with drawing out a future course of action & making decision in advance the most suitable course of actions for achieving fixed goals. According to KOONTZ, "Planning means making decision in advance i.e. what to do, when to do & how to do. It fills the hole from where we are & where we want to be". A plan means a course of actions for future. It is an application in solving problems & making decisions. Planning is purpose for courses of action to achieve the goals of the organization. Therefore, planning is a methodical thought about customs & means in order to achieve fixed goals. Planning is a compulsory activity to guarantee proper usage of human & object's resources. It is all in general, it is a knowledgeable action and it also helps in evading confusion, uncertainties, risks, wastages etc.

Organizing

It is the process of getting together physical, financial and human resources and developing relationship in productivity, amongst them for achieving goals of organization. Henry Fayol, said that "To establish an organization is to be provided with all useful or it's operative i.e. raw material, tools, capital and personnel's". To establish an organization involves responsiblity & providing human and material resources to the organizational structure. Organizing as a process includes:

- Finding the correct activities.
- Cataloging of group of activities.
- Duty assignment.
- Allocation of authority and construction of responsibility.
- Organizing authority and responsibility relations.

Staffing

It is the function of operating the structure of organization and keeping it operational. Recruitment has presumed greater importance in the recent years because of the development of technology, increase in business size, difficulty of human behavior etc. The main purpose of recruitment is to put right person on right job i.e. square pins in square holes and round pins in round holes. Kootz & O'Donell, both said that "Decision-making is a function of recruitment involves operating the structure of organization through proper and effective range; evaluation & growth of personnel to fill the roles planned UN the structure".

Recruitment involves: Manpower Planning (estimating man power in terms of searching, selecting the person and giving the right job).

- Staffing, choosing & Employment.
- Remuneration.
- Training & Development.
- Promotions & Transfer.
- Performance Appraisal.

Directing

It is a portion of administrative function which triggers the organizational methods to work efficiently to achieve goals of organization. It is considered as heart of the enterprise which sets it in motion the act of individuals because planning, organizing and staffing are the simple arrangements for finishing the job. Direction is that significant and dormant feature of management which deals straight with persuading, supervising, motivating other workers to achieve goals of organizational. Direction has following basics:

- Observation
- Communication
- Motivation
- Leadership

Supervision means it indicates superiors supervising the work of their subordinates. It is the act of inspecting & leading work & workers.

Motivation means it includes motivating, inspiring or encouraging the workers with passion to work. Motivations based on factors like being Optimistic, negative and incentives based on financial, non-financial may be used for this perseverance.

Leadership means a procedure which defined as, by which used by supervisors as guideline and impacts the job of workers in preferred direction.

Communications means a process of transcending information, view, knowledge etc. from one to another. It is a bond of understanding.

Controlling

The main purpose of having control is to guarantee that everything happens in traditional way with the principles. An efficient control system helps to calculate disorders before they actually happen. According to Theo Haimann, "It is the process of testing either or not standard progress is being made towards the objectives and goals and working if required, to change any deviation". According to Koontz & O'Donell "It is the size & adaptation of performance behavior of workers in order to make sure that the organization objectives and plans desired to acquire them as being achieved". Therefore these are the following steps of controlling:

- Formation of standard performance.
- Actual performance measurement.
- Educative action.
- Finding out any deviation by comparing of actual performance with the standards.

1.2. PRINCIPLES OF MANAGEMENT AND THEIR APPLICATION IN LIBRARIES

Division of Work

Henry Fayol's main principle for management defines that assigning jobs according to their specialties will increase staff performs at work. Therefore, the dividing of work into small jobs then becomes dominant. And so, specialization is significant because workers will do specific jobs not only for a single time but as a daily routine also. To an extent this is good. There are such departments of work in library and information centers. The Services Department for Readers' in library (commonly known as User Services, Customer Services, Public Services, etc.) distributes its major jobs into small departments and units. Not only has this fact been validated by other authors, it is also been proved to be valid to Technical Services Departments (Aguolu & Aguolu, 2002; Ifidon & Ifidon, 2007). Fayol, was certain in his department of work code in the sense that each and every jobs cannot be completed by all staff together at the same time. Moreover, effectiveness and efficiency of job are better reached if one worker is doing one job at a time and another doing a different job, but all leading to the same combined goal, at the same time. By this, output of work can be improved at the end of a time period, especially in a multipart organization where different types of outputs combined count for the overall productivity of the organization. Likewise, speaking about the logging room of a library for example, this principle also defines that as single or multiple persons register the books, another puts phone numbers in them and other will registers the titles as part of combing them as one and readying them to increase the flow wing. Even at that instance, other person at the exchange department may be creating place for their shelving, recording, etc. This is distribution of work and at the end of a day's work; the amount of jobs executed for the day can be more in number and it will be more significant than when every worker is grouped for every job fundamentals, one after another. Hence, workers are allotted with regular duties and are made to report that duty to superior every day.

However, as witnessed in modern libraries, some active librarians thinking of opposing to this as they, from time to time, reorganize staffs in a way that will give staff to new jobs. Unfavorably, the period of workers staying put in a certain post or office is becoming outdated, according to modern society nature. These points to the fact that in libraries, recent management practices are longer supporting these methods (Senge, 1990) and the causes are clear. First, in the library and information science occupation, the specialization practice in one department or aspect is not defined clearly as the best example. In case, this is obvious in the academic designations given to professors in the library and information department. Many of them are not settled to any particular library and information research area by their academic research title compared to what gathered in other engineering, science, and social science departments. As well, in the tutorial room, even at the degree of researcher level, research of scholars' will be more educational of their potential areas of specialization. But in current situation (operational in today's library and information center) it is rarely validated. This is one core subject against the library staffs remaining at a particular job for a long period and for others, all through their service period. After all that knowledge gaining in library and information science is distributed publically based on content and scope and thus be likely to produce male and female both can take up all type of job designed in the process of librarianship. So, library staffs who allowed remaining on a particular job schedule based on the reason of specialization may be decreasing efficiency of the job.

Again, concluding from study on the management style of 21st century, simplification in the design of the job is supported opposing to specialization. In service rendering organizations a study conducted to show how Western countries managers, design jobs that will be comfortable to all staff (Rodrigues, 2001). Therefore, not a single job design in modern organizations requires staffs specialized in subject core to perform. Working through the development of technologies, as it can also been seen at the introduction of library and information centers in the form of computers, automation, digitalization, etc. utilizing staffs as per their ability to use the machines to execute any job in the organization. But, this does not mean that there is no division of work. There are still formulas for division of work but the problem is that staffs are now managed to work in any division at any time because of the simplification of the work design. For example take the OPAC system: there may not be a need to have staffs tied to the job to categorizing workplace because of the OPAC system, as a typical platform of job design, will allow any staff from whichever department to add and/or erase content on the database of library. So, the managers of library and information centers should note the pattern shift from division of work by specialization to division of work by simplification.

Authority

This norm suggests that managers are needed to have authority in order to regulate workers to do the jobs while being responsible for their actions. This is both official and unofficial and is suggested for managers by Fayol. The decorum is in the expectation level of organization for the manager (his responsibilities), whereas the informality (the power) can be linked to the freedom of manager's command, instruct, employ and guarantee his or her responsibilities are performed effectively. Again, the two are like bread and butter on the manager: he must not abuse his power (authority). He must use it in good purpose with the equivalent responsibility. Thus, Fayol believed that since a manager must be responsible for his duties, he should as well have authority backing him up to accomplish his duties. This is correct and quite crucial to the success of organization.

This is the same case in library and information centers also. The staff in-Charge is accountable for the businesses of the library and has equivalent power to supervise it. Likewise, his or her assistants, head of the department, and unit officers are permitted the same in their respective dimensions. This makes the flow of work smoothly. But by implicating this, the respective sub-ordinates such as the assistant librarians, library officers, and others, in that case may be, become bottled up in the one-man idea cum direction of the library staff. Unfortunately, most head of the departments become so proud with their status, responsibility, and authority that they do not find it necessary to occasionally mingle and communicate with their staff. As the result, an cold relationship formed between related bad consequences, especially industrial conflict and reluctance of peoples to share knowledge (Ohadinma & Uwaoma, 2000). This may not be in the interests of the library given the saying that "two is better than one".

However, it is the new staffs that relate with the real-world jobs daily and are likely to constantly have something new in the field to teach them. Obviously, there is need for a managerial adjustment on this principle.

The stress should no longer be on influence to command workers. Reasonably, it should be encouraging staff's participation and motivation to take some initiatives. As the study by Blackburn and Rosen (1993) demonstrate that, award-winning organizations in the world use involved management and staff liberation against the authority and responsibility code. With this process, managers and their workers act more as controllers rather than rulers. Hence, library and information centers may not need a freak to control the management but rather an orchestra-type of leadership. Such leadership process will put up ideas, innovativeness, significant donations, and freedom to express from the junior staff to senior, which research has presented to have positive contributions to the growth and success of an organization (Blackburn & Rosen, 1993).

Discipline

This norm suggests for clear rules and regulations targeted to achieve good control over employees. Fayol must have seen the tendency of natural human to disorder. He observed the level of disorder in an organization may increase if employees are not strictly directed by rules, norms, and regulations from management. This is fact and has resulted in control over staffs in organizations. But in current situation, it has not been the finest method to achieve long-term order and goals of an organization. The scholars of management have seen that noble group participation and other kinds of casual unions are now taking the control in organizations (Mintzberg, 1973). The specific differences between staff dreaded by Fayol, which no doubt directed many organizations to failure because of a lack of official and mandatory organizational rules or weak and poorly forced programs of practice (Cavaleri & Obloj, 1993), are apparently attainable now through easygoing control systems. Union of workers and staff group is getting tougher and tougher on daily basis and has moral guiding system. In organizations where they are permitted to succeed, management is likely to have small or nothing to do on control over staffs. As well, they can make tough problems for managements who will not form a peaceful atmosphere for working with them. However, rather than being repressed by managements they have come to become stronger every day. Trade unionism by staff is, therefore, an element of the democratization of industrial organizations and government institutions because it provide for the attitudes and welfares of the worker while making certain decisions in management (Ohadinma & Uwaoma, 2000; Iwueke & Oparaku, 2011). Thus, the utilization of staffs or unions is an unceremonious control system. It can help organizations to maintain peace and sound. One secreted benefit is managements that approve this system have is that they save cost and time allotted to managerial discipline.

Similarly, in library and information centers, this system of discipline can be adopted. Librarians are to become less control in restraint rather than trying to impose rules and regulations of the institution at all cost. Active librarians can have fewer problems from staff rumors, gossip, and other forms of attack that usually come in the process of enforcing rules and regulations of institution. They can accomplish this in their libraries by trying the method of permitting workers to form group(s). For example, in a library an energetic junior executive group or senior executive group can go by a lengthy way to impose co-operation, union, belief, commitment, and order among its workers for the benefit of the library as an organization. As long as the maximum library management can give them is the free hand to exist, they will create some rules that can combine the organization of library more than it can divide it. In a subjective view it shows that libraries in which the workers and readers are happy with the level of love shown to them via visits, being emotional with them, etc. are such that have groups or unions in their library. This fact is braced by some reports in the textbook of management, which clearly propose that unions will help to maintain discipline among their staffs and maintain organization harmony (Imaga, 2001; Iwueke & Oparaku, 2011; Ohadinma & Uwaoma, 2000). Therefore, whereas some managers mistakenly thinks that unions are formed to oppose management and making demands unnecessarily, library and information managers should see that unions can nelp the organization to achieve order and maintain discipline. This will show the real reason and remove the fear of their existence.

Unity of Command

This principle suggests that only one plan should be there and one goal and one leader for each of the plans. Obviously, organization functions are based on well-known objectives (Drucker, 1954). But, this should not be misunderstood with departments and units who apparently have their explicit objectives. Fayol was saying is that an organization will certainly have dominant objectives which need to be followed and as well departmental and unit goals which also need to be reached in order to meet the unified objective.

Library and information centers are mainly formed to gain and manage the world of source for information and provide information services to their users. But also, from departments and units they will have other objectives; occasionally it differs from each other. This is in route with the job conditions and abnormal work routines of each of the various sub-systems of the library (Edoka, 2000; Nnadozie, 2007). However, the actions of each department or unit are targeted at library's auxiliary central objective of giving users the information services. And for each of the departments to accomplish its objectives, they establish and follow various plans (not a single plan). So Henri Fayol's original proposal is that one plan should be pursued by one head only is no longer reasonable. For example, the Transmission Department of the library has to provide service offering and also record library users. Does it mean that it will have separate heads because of the different assignments involved? No; it is true that plans are different, and in this case, one is set for how to register users and the other strategizes how to lend out library materials to people and ensure that they return them, or be responsible for not returning them on time or at all. However, it does not call for a split-up in the job in terms of leadership. Rather, what managers of library should maintain on is goals and plans of the department should be followed in an organized method, so that there won't be any necessary for designated leader in each plan of group action. This method of management is already in action on most of the libraries in Africa where few individuals are used to carry out multiple tasks due to unavailability of staff (Ifidon, 1979 & 1985).

Subordination of Individual Interests to Organization's Interests

The interest of staff (individual or in group) is surpassed by interests of the organization. Therefore, for the well-being of the organization staffs need to sacrifice all their individual interests. In other words, staffs that are not dedicated to the objectives of the organization cannot be tolerated by the organization and command even if it is to the disadvantage of personal and family interests. In following organizational or commercial success this is one hard way. It may have worked earlier but now, but it is not unique any longer due to some reasons. Starting from, Mayor (1933) and McGregor (1960) have exposed that staffs can do their work better, when they are valued and shown a reasonable sense of being in the right place. Second, organizations are submissive to the discrepancy of change. They change their objectives based on the situation and expect their staff to adjust to the changes quickly. And, one of the quickest ways to get staff to adjust and obey with changes in organization is to participate in the interest of the staffs. Which means, staff training and rehabilitation, which is the most cost-effective method for managen ent, and it is not only an investment in the staff to procure but also a promise to staff personal development. During these training sessions, sta:f enjoys several benefits such as security for their job, payment of salaries, full support, and other payments that makes staff pleased and encouraged to put in their finest in action when they return from the training program.

The application of this standard should not be forced in library and information centers. Library managers and administrators must learn to make staff work happily. Staffs are happy, will always put in all their best at work. Ways of keeping staff motivated to work happily include, from time to time, showing a commitment to staff both directly and indirectly. Proper commitments can come from supporting staff to further training, short development courses, sessions, and meetings. Some informal commitments include leave support packages for staff, open and consistent communication, and flexibility to staff personal requests. Library managers and administrators also use these formal and informal incentives to show their staff a sense of belonging, thereby making them more productive (Ifidon & Ifidon, 2007). For instance, a staff member permitted to leave office early to pick up her children from school will be glad and, more often than not, reciprocate by a commitment to work during the periods she will be at work. On the contrary, a member that is not permitted to attend to such personal needs and is regimented to the opening and closing hours of work at the library may sit back in his office all day achieving nothing. If a psychological test is conducted on this case, the result may likely show that the latter staff member achieved nothing in the office, not primarily because he wanted to pay back the manager by not working, but more because he was not able to concentrate at work and even when he tried he could not focus because of where his mind was; this is especially so if the family need for which the excuse is denied is crucial. Productive library administrators ensure that an environment is created for staff to have a sense of appreciation, especially when they have some personal needs. Staff with such a sense of appreciation or recognition tend to put in their best in the discharge of their work and pursuit of the library's corporate goals (Aguolu & Aguolu, 2002). Thus, while it was held before that staff should give up their interests for the organization, now the reverse is the case. This means that organizations commit itself to the interest of the staff so that they can be more productive and committed to the objectives of the organization.

Remuneration

Payment of staff salaries should be as deserved. The salary should be reasonable to both staff and management and neither party should be short-changed. The salary of every staff member must be justifiable. A supervisor should receive more pay than line staff. Thus, whosever management appoints to be supervisor takes more than the subordinates by virtue of his or her responsibilities. It does not really matter whether a subordinate works harder and is more productive than the supervisor. As long as management does not promote the subordinate he continues to receive lesser pay to what his boss gets even as he works more than his boss. The above generally encapsulates Fayol's position on remuneration.

However, this approach to the administration of the reward system is gradually giving way in contemporary library management practice. There is a noticeable modification in the application of this principle as it is arbitrary in nature (Ohadinma & Uwaoma, 2000). It is quite agreed that it will be inappropriate for a subordinate to receive more pay than his boss. So, management researchers have complemented Fayol's notion with a new modifications arguing that this system of remuneration discourages hard work and productivity (Cascio, 1987). As a result, the "performance based pay system" recommended by Wallace and Fay (1988) is what is used nowadays. This pay system supports the idea that organizations should design a performance scale with which staff should be evaluated. Imperatively, productive staffs get promoted and take more salary than non-productive staff. In a way also, this was Taylor's (1911) idea that has just re-surfaced. Taylor's idea supports hard work and extra commitment from the staff. His notion was that the more output from an employee, the more pay he receives. So, with this modification, every staff member receives a salary based on his or her measured output.

In present day library and information centers, this productivity measurement scale is adopted. In fact, the performance-based pay system is almost the norm everywhere. The only problem with some libraries and other information-related organizations is that they do not publish and/or orientate their staff on the measurement scaling or promotion criteria. Staff need to understand the criteria and have free access to the document. More so, library managers should as a matter of morality be just in the productivity measurement. Most librarians discourage their hardworking staff or make them resign for another job as they usually envy some member's speed of productivity and promotion. Some library managers and their deputies are in the habit of comparing the number of years a hardworking and productive staff member has spent on the job with the many years some lazy and unproductive staff have given on the same job as a reason for why the former should not rise faster or even above the latter. This point has been raised in some library science textbooks where non-adherence to the principles of the performance-based reward system has been faulted (Aguolu & Aguolu, 2002 ; Edoka, 2000). Library managers should, therefore, avoid sentiments and award promotions to whoever has worked for them as many times as their hard work qualifies them. This is crucial if a library must retain the best staff and survive in a highly competitive information environment.

Centralization

This principle suggests that decision-making should be centralized. This means that decision-making and dishing-out of orders should come from the top management (central) to the middle management, where the decisions are converted into strategies and are interpreted for the line staffs who execute them (decentralization). This is still working in many organizations. Library and information centers also apply this principle. For instance, it is conventional for the Librarian-in-Charge to hold meetings with deputies and/ or departmental heads to initiate broad policy guidelines while the deputies and departmental heads take management decisions to their departments and units where they are finally executed and monitored (Ifidon & Ifidon, 2007). Nonetheless, management researchers have found another system which is working for many western organizations. Blackburn and Rosen (1993) observe that successful organizations in the United States of America (USA) apply a group decision making and implementation system. This means that units and departments make decisions and strategize their implementation based on their task, control focus, and job specifics.

Bringing this to the library may nevertheless not be so clear, especially in the beginning. But if it can be tried, it means that library departments will be empowered to meet weekly or monthly, and to make decisions as relating to their department, design their jobs, and draw their roster and schedule of duty. Later on, the decisions and plans of the department will be forwarded to the Librarian-in-Charge for immediate input and approval. Such a system of decision making allows for innovativeness and broad thinking among staff of all levels and also allows the Librarian to be less burdened with the library's daily complaints. As well, librarians can have time to attend the numerous institutions' meetings which they are statutory members of by reason of their position. However, it should be noted that the group decision making system cannot survive in bureaucracy—a system where mails are delayed for long. The Librarian must be committed to treating mail every day. In his absence, he should appoint someone to deputize him. This is because the work group decision-making system requires management to approve or make input to the group's decision before they can commence work. Take for instance where the Digital Library Department of a library has met and taken a decision to be closed to users for three days to enable them to embed an anti-pornography firewall on their server system in order to save it from unauthorized downloads that may crash the server. The decision mail reached the Librarian's desk and for many days it was yet to be treated. Although oral communication to the Librarian can be faster in this case, in a management system where records are necessary for actions, the Librarian's delay in treating the mail would not do any good to the group's decision. So, while the system is good, it requires promptness on actions from both management and staff. Thus, Fayol's 'principle of centralization' is like a trickle-down decision flow, routing decisions from top to the bottom. But the work group decision system suggested therein is a bottom-up movement, which allows the staff to initiate ideas and job specific decisions for the organization.

Scalar Chain

This principle is a product of the formal system of organization. It is also known as the hierarchy principle.

It asserts that communication in the organization should be vertical only. It insists that a single uninterrupted chain of authority should exist in organizations. Horizontal communication is only allowed when the need arises and must be permitted by the manager. This vertical organizational and communication arrangement is the conventional practice in most library and information centers where orders and similar directives flow from the Librarian-in- Charge to the Deputy Librarians, to the Departmental Heads, and to the Unit or Sectional Heads, respectively (Edoka, 2000 ; Nnadozie, 2007). This is a four-layer hierarchy. It is neither twelve nor three layers, as Braham (1989) argues that a three-layer organizational hierarchy does better and faster than a twelve-layer hierarchy. Also, it has been shown in research that US-based organizations that practiced one-layer hierarchy systems recorded far better results than others that operated three-layer systems and above (Hinterhuber & Popp, 1992). Nowadays, a horizontal or flat management hierarchy system is advocated against the vertical order canvassed by Henri Fayol. The argument is that the former helps organizations to take decisions and implement them faster without unnecessary bottlenecks, contrary to what is observed in the later. Should this be applied in library and information centers, the implication is that the relatively vertical hierarchy order in most libraries should be displaced with the flat or horizontal hierarchy system. Figure 1 is a comparative illustration of a typical vertical organizational structure and the horizontal alternative being proposed.

Based on the above illustration, coupled with the new management findings that a horizontal organizational hierarchy allows for faster decision making and implementation than the vertical order system, library and information centers may have to operate a horizontal hierarchy system (Fig. 2 Diagram B) henceforth. The present system of having divisional heads, departmental

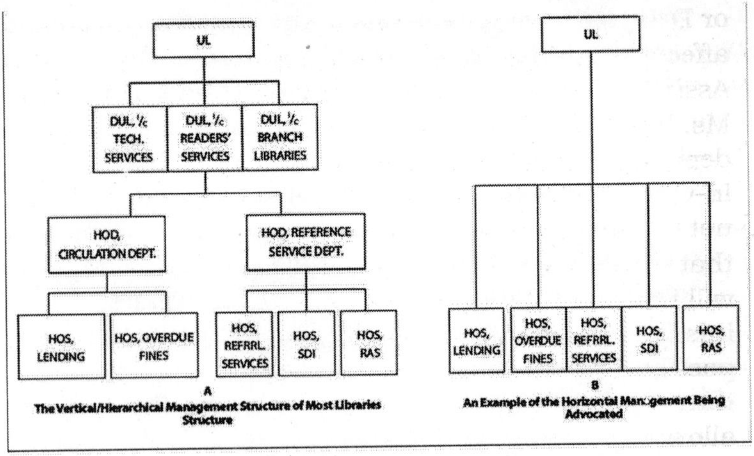

Fig. 2. Scalar chain diagram illustrating Fayol's vertical order and the proposed horizontal order

heads, and in some cases, unit or sectional heads also (Fig. 2 Diagram A), may have to give way for a flat order where it will only be the Librarian-in-Charge and, most directly, the unit/sectional heads (as per specific job element or focus). However, this may not be welcomed by librarians in some institutions and countries where the deputy and departmental heads positions attract office allowances and other appurtenances. Yet, we must be realistic; such ladders on the management chart may not be helpful for library organization in the nearest future. But, this one thing can be done also: break down the vertical order (Diagram A) into a flat order (Diagram B), increase the Sections/Units based on job specifics and call them Departments (which is more conventional), and redistribute the office heads in the initial vertical order to head the departments. This way, the fear of losing office/headship allowances and other benefits is averted. The beauty of the horizontal organization being advocated lies in its adaptability to the peculiar needs of both small and large libraries (Ifidon & Ifidon, 2007). Besides, most library staff are at home with its flexibility bearing in mind that positions attained by promotion (such as Senior Librarian or Deputy Librarian positions), are not in any way to be affected in the horizontal system. Hence, Mr. A can be an Assistant Librarian by grade and heads a department while Ms. B can be a Deputy Librarian by grade, also heading a department. Both of them report directly to the Librarian-in-Chief. Yet, the grade level and rank status of both is not the same and cannot be the same just on the grounds that both of them are departmental heads. Of course, there will be no problem with the remuneration system also as it is based on performance scale (grade level) and not on positional status (the headship privilege). The only thing that may be the same in this case is the headship allowance, if it is across the board for all staff grades. But, the normal annual salary (remuneration) due for each departmental head is purely determined according to grade levels and as such will vary among the heads.

Order

This is another formal organizational control system which has been interpreted in different ways. Some see it as the rule of giving every material its right position in the organization and others think that it means assigning the right job to the right employee (Rodrigues, 2001). Whichever is the case, library and information centers must keep every information material in the right place and as well assign staff to jobs that suit them. A Library Assistant is not expected to handle the office and responsibilities of a Senior Librarian. This is because, among other things, their qualifications, job schedule, and remunerations are clearly different (Ifidon, 1985; Ifidon & Ifidon, 2007). However, buttressing more on the first suggested meaning of Henri Fayol's 'principle of order,' it is true that information resources in the library should be kept in the right place. Here, what makes a place right is the ease of access and use it avails the users. Let us take the location of offices for example. In a library complex of two or three floors, the office of Librarian has no convenience in being located at any of the offices at the upper floors. Visitors to the Librarian's office, who have nothing to do with the readings halls and other departments, have no business passing through or across them before they can access the Librarian's office. The Librarian's office should be located on the ground floor where visitors and users can access it easily. Likewise, the porter stand should be accessible to users immediately when they enter the library. This is the prevailing practice in the Nigerian university system in West Africa as most of the library briefs are in line with this proposal (Ifidon, 1985; Ifidon & Ifidon, 2007; Ononogbo, 2008). Users do not have to walk to one point to keep their bags and down to another point before they can enter the library.

In fact, if library and information centers must comply with this principle of order, it must be looked at from a more holistic point of view. For instance, taking a look at the present structure of offices and demarcations of most library buildings in Nigeria, the principle of order is practically compromised. This is in spite of the good suggestions in the available librarians' and architects' briefs for the construction of library buildings (Ifidon, 1985; Ifidon & Ifidon, 2007; Ononogbo, 2008). In a library that wants to infuse order right from the design of its work environment, the transparent partitioning system, as seen in Banks, is ideal for adoption. Nowadays, organizations operate the open office system. An open office is that in which there is little or no privacy as the only partition between offices could be just transparent glass walls. In some cases, dwarf walls or wooden boards are used. The major benefit of this arrangement is that it enhances transparency and ventilation (Idih, Njoku, & Idih, 2011). Staff can see themselves from their offices. The users can see them as well too.

The Readers' Services Departments of the library and their officers are the most likely to adopt this system of office sitting/demarcation. It allows the head of the department to see his staff and users also while they too see them. In this case, there will hardly be room for staff that do unethical things in the library such as sleeping, eating, and gossiping in the office. Likewise, users will be more cautious while in the library because staff from various offices can be watching them. In fact, the transparent partitioning of library staff offices will intuitively drive staff to work and not to relax or chat away during official hours. However, this transparent partitioning system should not be open to users in the case of Technical Departments. But within the technical departments, the offices should be transparent too so that staff can see themselves. These are some important elements of order which could be modified to suit the peculiar needs of libraries.

Equity

Another word for equity is fairness. Henri Fayol suggested that managers should be fair to their staff. But the fairness required, probably, is such that must make staff to comply with principle No. 6 - subordination of individual interests to organizational interests – which does not lead to desired productivity in organizations nowadays. As suggested earlier under principle No. 6 in this paper, the system of organization that flourishes in today's society is such that accommodates staff and owns them up, as it were. Such organizations make staff feel at home, share a portion of profits with staff, communicate with staff, remain open to staff, share staff feelings, and identify with staff personal/family challenges. This is the type of organization that succeeds these days. Managers of library and information centers can apply these strategies in their relationships with members of staff. Where they do, they will avoid all forms of partiality, treat all staff equally, deny no staff promotions, and encourage weak staff to shape up. More so, they advise staff regularly on how to grow on the job, mentor staff, avoid favouritism, build up an unbiased attitude, and disallow gossip. Staff of the library are rewarded or punished based strictly on their commitment, faithfulness, and productivity and not on either friendship or filial relationships (Ohadinma & Uwaoma, 2000). This means that openness to all and even-handedness are integral parts of the key to attaining equity in organizations. So, library managers should rather address issues relating to staff before them and not at their backs. In all, impartiality is the kernel of this principle. As a result, it must be upheld by library managers not only in the interests of the library as an organization, but also for their own good since observation has shown that impartial managers are respected and appreciated by their staff.

Stability of Personnel Tenure

In this principle, Fayol expresses the need to recruit the right staff and train them on the job with a hope to retain them for long. The basis of this principle is the belief that such staff with a secured tenure will put back into the organization the knowledge and experience which they may have garnered in the course of working for the organization. This, however, is considered an old-fashioned way of approaching management. Contemporary management is suggesting the recruitment of staff that are already-made with experience and with the right qualifications. Some organizations have gone further to downsize staff recruited in the old system because of their unwillingness to adapt to new ways of performing jobs in the organization. As a matter of fact, new generation organizations are not merely keen in recruiting men and women whom they will invest much in from the start in order to get them working for the organization. However, they are willing to spend on staff members that already have high success profiles and experience so that they can develop the organization all the more. So, this is the era of recruiting the best qualified staff. The idea is that work can be very productive from the start and afterwards the staff can be trained to improve on what they already know how to do. This is one side of the principle and library and information centers managers should take note of it.

Another angle of Fayol's 'principle of stability of tenure' is that staff should be retained for as long as possible, sometimes up to retirement. But, this is not the order of the day in recent times, as mobility of labour is becoming the culture of many workers. For one, workers believe in having several opportunities—that new jobs can offer such things as better pay, job satisfaction, promotions, job security, societal recognition, and others. But this is not healthy forlibrary and information centers. Brain drain is a factor that should be avoided. In fact, library and information centers should hold firm on Fayol's principle here. Staff should be developed via on the job training, seminars, conferences, mentoring, and further studies. Organizational culture is not always easy to transmit and retain (Shein, 1984) let alone a system to change workers often. The majority of the new workers coming are often from another organization with a different culture. So, managers of library and information centers should retain Fayol's 'principle of stability of personnel tenure' but must avoid recruiting into the library men and women who will not be productive to the system until they are trained. An element of this is noticeable in the head-hunting and recruitment of subject-specialists by authorities of special libraries. Although this calibre of staff may be new when they report or resume, they have had previous exposure and experience in the public or private sectors (Nnadozie, 2007). When staffs are recruited from other establishments, the direct and indirect costs involved in training staff upon employment should therefore be avoided. This, however, does not eliminate the need for on the job mentoring essential for both new and old staff.

Initiative

A good manager must be one who can be creative to initiate new ideas and also be able to implement them. Fayol was direct to managers at this point. He understood the importance of good ideas to the growth and success of organizations. But, on the contrary, he did not foresee the situation of today where staffs are becoming the idea-banks of organizations. This has been observed in Western countries where group problem-solving systems are patronized against dependence on top level management as the problem-solving point (Magjuka, 1991 & 1992). Moreover, Mintzberg's study in his PhD research (Robinson, 2005) confirmed that managers of these days seem not to be very good in initiating and implementing ideas as they are often preoccupied with so many other related and unrelated commitments that, in the end, leave them running after "work current, specific, well-defined and non-routine" activities. So, it is advisable for managers to empower their staff and give them the level playing ground required to initiate and implement new ideas.

In library and information centers, the almost non-existence of new ideas among librarians (especially in developing countries) has made library organization seem uncreative, stagnant, and old-fashioned. This is the reason why their library customers, especially adolescents and young adults, are resorting to the Internet, since there is nothing new in the library. Whereas the Internet and its accompanying technologies offer a lot of platforms for proactive librarians to work with and retain their customers, a good number of library staff and their managers are rather not systematic and reflective planners. It may be that staffs are waiting for the Librarian for initiatives and the Librarians-in-Charge, as managers, are preoccupied with numerous other things. This should not continue if the library organization hopes to avoid decline and liquidation (Ohadinma & Uwaoma, 2000). Administrators and managers of library and information centers therefore should imbue their subordinates with the confidence to create and develop new ideas, as well as to implement them. Rewards and encouragements should be there for creative and/or innovative staff members so that generation of ideas can become competitive to the glory of the management and for the good of the organization as a collective body.

Esprit de Corps

This is a French phrase which means enthusiasm and devotion among a group of people. Fayol is of the view that organization's should enforce and also maintain high morale and unity among their staff. This is imperative as the existence of an organization is a result of the coming together of men and women under a collective interest. Thus, understanding, love for each other, unity, peace, and common determination is paramount to their success. The saying that united we stand, divided we fall is equally applicable in libraries and information centers. In the same manner, managers of library and information centers must ensure that the library organization is characterized by staff unity and co-operation. This however does not mean that some staff members will not disagree or quarrel. It is natural with some human beings to quarrel once in a while. But library managers must be strategists in such cases to ensure that such misunderstandings amongst staff do not affect common goals of the library organization.

1.3. INTRODUCTION OF SCIENTIFIC MANAGEMENT

Scientific Management for Public Libraries, it begins with a definition of the relevant terms and concepts, then reviews briefly the main possible methods and techniques, and finally suggests some future possibilities. Subsequent articles in this issue deal in detail with various aspects of the subject.

Definition of Terms

Needless to say, "scientific management" cannot be usefully defined in a short sentence. This is partly because it embraces many different potential areas of emphasis, and partly because it represents a type of thinking which, although well known for over half a century, is still developing, and partly because it has varying implications and applications for different kinds of work. The present consideration of scientific management stresses those features which are most appropriate to public libraries, and which are general in nature. If scientific management means anything more than common sense, its significance lies in what science has to contribute to common-sense findings?

We are all familiar with and recognize as desirable certain hallmarks of science, e.g., a detachment and objectivity which overrides passion or prejudice, a penchant for quantitative measures which allow for precision, and care in defining terms and in using such terms only as defined. There are, however, three qualities of science which are not always either recognized or accepted, and which are of particular importance ir the application of scientific management in public libraries. The first is that the method of science calls for an awareness and a painful sensitivity to the assumptions underlying the reascning on which an investigation or study rests. An assumption is a proposition as to the relationship between two or more factors which is not known Mr. Goldhor is Chief Librarian of the Evansville, Indiana, Public Library.

Scientific Management in Public Libraries

Scientific Management in Public Libraries to be either true or false but which is stated as though it were true. In a world which is for practical purposes infinite in its range of undiscovered truths, the finite nature of man's knowledge makes it necessary for him always to act on the basis of assumptions or else not to act at all. The use of assumptions is neither good nor bad, if they are recognized for what they are. The danger is that a proposition originally introduced as an assumption may come in time to be treated as proven fact, when perhaps its truth has never even been tested, let alone established. Langer shows very nicely how our very language, in the questions we put, sets limits to our answers by the assumptions on which it rests.

One of the early signs of progress in a scientific investigation appears when one can begin to formulate the "right" questions to ask. In large part this turns on a critical awareness of the crucial assumptions, and it is often fruitful to consider alternate or opposite assumptions and then see what logically follows. Thus, for example, is it actually true that patrons of public libraries need, want, or tend to seek author, title, and subject entries in a card catalog? Do fines for overdue books actually serve to bring books back faster, or even as fast, as other possible devices or none at all? Do library employees more often take jobs elsewhere because of higher pay than because of other, and correctible, working conditions?

The great virtue of being conscious of one's assumptions, of examining them carefully, of considering alternates, and of testing the most crucial propositions, instead of "assuming" what the truth is-the great virtue of these acts is that they enlarge one's mental horizon considerably and open up problems to many more approaches than are otherwise available. At one time, for instance, it was generally thought necessary that in public libraries all books be kept on closed shelves. The theory on which that belief rested (e.g., that people would steal the books, or at least seriously disarrange them) was challenged by some librarians who had no direct proof of the falsity of the assumptions but who were willing to take the risks involved in abandoning them. It should be recognized that following out contrary suppositions does not guarantee success, but merely increases the number of possible lines of action, some of which are likely to be ineffective. But anyone who does not count on having some failures in the use of the scientific method, for a diversity of reasons, is likely to be disillusioned earlier rather than later. The successful application of scientific management depends, more than on any other single factor, on the ability of the investigator to pursue his study in the light of the widest possible number of alternatives. And this is all the more important in librarianship because many of the assumptions on which library practice rests deal with factors which are variables and not constants; thus an assumption may be true at one time in history and not necessarily at another.

A second major quality of science which is important in this context is its dependence on theory. All science embraces accurate observation, but not all accurate observation is synonymous with science. The differentiating characteristic is the presence or absence of a theoretical approach which serves to give direction to the work of observation and to allow for its analysis and interpretation. If observation without theory is sterile, theory without observation is useless for operational purposes. The net result of observation should be the revision of the theory which initiated the observation. Thus it is that the cycle of theory, observation, and reformulation of theory makes science ever dynamic and ever subject to self-improvement.

It probably is easy to see how the cycle works and works beneficially; the difficulty is in generating the initial theory, which is as true in other fields as in librarianship. The need to fill the gap is one of the reasons we keep coming back to attempts at a philosophy of librarianship. Actually, however, for practical purposes and for use in scientific management, it is probably enough to deal in terms of hypotheses rather than of theory. The difference between a hypothesis and a theory is basically the difference between the specific and the general. A theory is an attempt to explain in as general terms as feasible the nature of as large a group of phenomena as possible. Any one theory may give rise to a potentially infinite number of hypotheses, each of which is an attempt to restate a part of the theory in more specific terms and with reference to a smaller group of instances. By definition, a good hypothesis is one which is so stated as to point to the data which need to be gathered by observation, in order to test the truth or falsity of the hypothesis and in turn increase or diminish faith in the general theory.

The habit of thinking in terms of hypotheses is likely to be of considerable value to librarians, especially in attempting to apply scientific management. To ask such a question as "How can I develop a circulation system better than the one I have now?" is not very useful. To rephrase the question as a hypothesis-using such stilted language as one quickly abandons after developing a few hypotheses one might reasonably embark on a study to ascertain whether photographic charging is faster in recording the withdrawal of books than is any other known scheme. Now notice that this hypothesis clearly involves a supposition that speed in charging books is an important, if not the most important, element in a superior charging system. It also seems to reflect a general theory as to the nature of the operation of public libraries, else why pursue this line of approach? Third, it narrows the subject down to a small but manageable scope. And finally, it points clearly to the body of data which must be ascertained in order to restate the hypothesis as a proposition of tested truth, to revise it, or to discard it as untrue.

All applications of scientific management of any consequence can be rephrased in such terms, and they will be more successful if initially they are so conceived and executed. Just as consideration of alternative assumptions is no guarantee of fruitful results, so use of a hypothesis may produce negative effects. To use a hypothesis means by definition that one is committed to test its truth or falsity. He does not set out to make a case for it, which would be to operate on the basis of a prejudice. The value of a hypothesis lies not in its being used to screen out data unfavorable to it, but in its help to the investigator in deciding which facts are relevant and how to interpret them after they are collected. In large part the hypothesis performs its function by forcing the investigator to think carefully about a problem before beginning to collect data.

The third aspect of science which is highly relevant to its use in scientific management is implicit in the goal which science strives to attain. Science starts with attempting to comprehend a phenomenon and then proceeds inexorably to achieve control over what it is examining. It cannot begin without clear, complete, and precise descriptions; it cannot advance without understanding the "how." But so far science is passive. It comes into its own when it can make correct predictions as to what will happen when specific factors are brought together in certain ways and under given conditions. It has nothing left to achieve when it can make correct predictions in quantitative terms as to the results of minute variations in any factor or any environmental conditions; and that is what is meant by control. Similarly scientific management is concerned not alone with getting results; after all, as good or better results have been and can be secured by trial and error, by insight, or even by guess or luck. But what nothing else has ever been able to do as well, and as consistently, and over as broad a range of problems, is to predict the future, and especially to do so in measurable terms based on known initial variations.

Another way of saying all this is that a prime function of science is to distinguish between correlation and causation. Now it is true that if X causes Y, then X will be correlated with Y; but it is also true that when X and Y happen to be correlated it may be not at all clear whether X causes Y, Y causes X, both are caused by Z, or the correlation is the result of chance alone. Probably the single greatest difficulty in science is to ascertain causation between two factors. Suffice it to say that one test, and the most conclusive one, of our knowledge of causation is the ability to predict correctly the response elicited by a given stimulus. The development of science in this respect-from a concern with description to a mastery of control-is dearly evidenced in the history of scientific management; and future developments in scientific management are sure to emphasize ascertaining the causal relationship in any given problem. It is useful in this connection always to state a hypothesis with a causal element in it, to explain why the relationship expressed is deemed to hold true.

So far we have considered only the "scientific" part of scientific management, and indeed the historical role of the second half of the term has simply been to limit the field of application of the scientific method. Scientific management, as a body of principles and techniques, constitutes a sort of applied science which already is spilling over in its applications to other areas than those of management (in the sense of administration) and of production, and this is a trend which probably will continue and grow. However, consideration of scientific management is focused here and now primarily on those applications in libraries which pertain to activities other than public service.

Such a distinction is one of convenience, however, rather than integral or necessary, and reflects the usual line of historical development. By scientific management is meant here the study of work operations, both those common in other institutions generally and those peculiar to libraries, in order to control them. This definition approximates the usual understanding of the term and identifies the area in which most activity is currently proceeding in public libraries. For practical purposes it excludes certain subjects which are potentially subject to such study, such as the service functions of public libraries, experimentation in public library activities, democratic administration, and community analysis. Just as scientific management surely will extend its application to these other fields in time, so too wherever it is used it tends to move from naive considerations of economy, to those of efficiency, to those of control on behalf of any given quality or combination of qualities.

The Main Possible Methods and Techniques

The possible procedures in scientific management are numerous. New techniques are constantly being devised, and all techniques need constantly to be scrutinized for their relevance to the problem at hand. The classical type of study is that of time and motion, utilizing the stop watch and motion picture, but this has very limited application in public libraries. In general, the main techniques of scientific management useful in public libraries can be conveniently grouped under two headings. There are those which deal with what might loosely be called policies, and may never be represented by anything more than a statement on paper, and others which have to do with changes in physical layout and in actual work operations.

All techniques of scientific management are likely to have their results expressed at one point or another in written documents, and in many instances they can find expression in no other way. It is this latter group which, in relation to libraries, now is to be considered. It is a large and heterogeneous collection, all the more so because library procedures involve a large component of paper work and because traditionally paper work has received less attention than machine production of goods, for example. The techniques to be discussed here are only a sample of those available; not all of them are recommended, and certainly new and better ones are sorely needed.

One of the more general techniques which find expression primarily only in written reports, and which is used or useful in public libraries, is the survey. Library surveys range from long, expensive, and discerning studies to short, inexpensive, and superficial reviews. They vary in scope from the most comprehensive to the most specialized. They may be based on extensive, factual examination, or on little more than subjective impressions. They often are occasioned by motives irrelevant to scientific management: and in any event they incorporate no methods or techniques peculiar to themselves. Hence a library survey as such is valuable for scientific management only if the person in charge has a better mind than the chief of the library surveyed, or if he utilizes other more specific techniques which are equally available to all to use. Both these conditions are found in some instances, but the survey technique in general is probably not a particularly useful tool in scientific management.

On a lower level of generality, there has been all too little study and development of techniques with a view to formulation and application of specific institutional objectives. The basic consideration is simply that a library which doesn't know where it is going and where it wants to go is Lkely to supply ineffective answers to the problems of its age. Goals, clearly stated in operational terms, may specify the areas and the direction ir' which improvement by means of scientific management is needed. How to evaluate and state library objectives is not easy to describe, but their basic necessity for purposes of improvement in work is becoming ever clearer and more fully recognized. All too many specific activities in public libraries would be greatly changed, or eliminated, if a set of precise aims were available by which to check their validity. Then too a library's goals, if properly stated, can serve to indicate the type of control which one would seek to achieve through scientific management, e.g., whether to put first speed in charging books, or immediate knowledge of the whereabouts of every book.

The usefulness of library goals lies not in their statement but in their use. They supposedly determine policies, and policies find expression in work procedures. Measurement of the results of work activities then may be used to review and revise procedures and policies in the light of the aims. The review of the objectives themselves is usually called evaluation, and is another story. A library's goals normally will be used initially in planning, both short range and long range; and planning potentially affects all other operations, for to plan is "to 'walk out to meet the future' and mold it to the pattern of our dreams." The techniques of planning are many and useful, but are derived mainly from experience with programs for buildings, with budgets, and with the control and coordination of materials as on an assembly line. The techniques for planning the development of an adult education program, for example, are less well understood. We are badly in need of case studies, of the "capture-and-record" type, of planning for libraries.

The administrative organization of an institution is the most general subject in connection with which techniques of scientific management for public libraries are well known. By administrative organization is meant the grouping of responsibilities and functions into formally designated units in order to carry out the purposes and goals of an institution. Logically the organization of a public library should mirror its aims; 19 actually most public libraries have an organization which has developed in the course of time on a haphazard basis, by the simple accretion of new organizational units to handle new functions. Thus it is that library surveys tend to consider the organization of the institution, since there is usually so much room for improvement. Some of the common principles of administrative organization, which are often violated in public libraries, are:

1. The span of control should be kept short.
2. Responsibility for any one function or service should be clearly allocated and not diffused.
3. Homogeneous functions or services should be unified, and an organizational unit should be assigned one or related functions and not unrelated ones.
4. Adequate provision should be made for staff and auxiliary as well as for line or operating functions.
5. Administrative organizations should be reviewed periodically.

There are various techniques for the analysis and improvement of administrative organization, such as preparation and publication of an organizational chart, authorization of lines of technical advice as well as channels of command, creation of devices to secure and improve coordination (as exemplified for libraries in the role of the coordinators in the Enoch Pratt Free Library)? use of specialists in place of generalists in the administrative hierarchy, and the development of more levels in the organization as the institution grows in size (as instanced in the regional branch libraries in Chicago). All this points to unsolved problems and unanswered questions in the field of public library administration. For example, is it necessarily true, as military authorities say, that a staff officer cannot also perform line functions? Do the usual principles of administrative organization, tested and proven in large organizations, apply equally to small libraries?

Personal Administration

Personnel administration is another large and important area in which public libraries are beginning to use devices of scientific management and are sure to profit by it. Probably the single most important technique here is that of the position-classification plan. The essential principles for the correct use of this involve a job analysis, provision for continual review, emphasis on the duties assigned and not on the qualitications of any particular or present employee, and recognition of the relationship with a salary schedule and of the other potential measures utilizing a position-classification plan. Like most techniques of scientific management, the position-classification plan can be devised by an outside group or by a library administration and staff; given a minimum level of competence, which can be developed, the latter method is likely to be more successful in winning acceptance for the scheme and in securing continuing attention to the results of its operation.

Other techniques of scientific management in this area deal with such matters as salary standardization, improvement of working conditions (in regard to light, noise, fatigue), systematic in-service training, and employee turnover. In connection with personnel administration, it is clear that scientific management needs to be designed for ends other than simple and immediate economy. Thus, elimination of employee turnover probably is not a desirable objective at which to aim. Not to be excluded from this field, but still awaiting development for the most part, is the whole vast field of democratic administration.

1.4. MANAGEMENT INFORMATION SYSTEM

Introduction

The term Management Information System (MIS) is of relatively recent origin and is widely adopted following the accelerated use of computers in the early 1960's. The Management Information System to business what is the nervous system is to the human body. It is described as "informational blood stream" of an organisation. It encompasses a wide range of subject matters like management theory, communication theory, human processing of data and information technology. Often the concept of Management Information System is splintered and confused by' touting new ideas like decision support system, management reporting system, office information system, transaction processing systems, office automation, information resource management and database management system as replacements for Management Information System. However, a brood interpretation of the concept of Management Information System includes all the above.

Management Information System has something significantly to do with two important management functions (or elements of management) studied in Unit 1, namely, planning and controlling. The basis for Management Information System is that computers, in addition to data processing, can serve as fine tools to improve the planning and control of operations by providing better information for decision making. As library and information professionals, we provide information support for research, education, planning, business, decision making and so on and so forth. By and large, libraries are providing information from public domain published information and to a limited extend public domain semi-published information. The critical requirements in a decision making situation in business is the classified and unpublished information as well as the crucial dynamic internally generated information. Each business enterprise will design and maintain its own Management Information System for the purpose and library and information professionals with their techniques and tools can play vital role in this endeavour. However, the purpose of this 'unit is to seek answer to the questions like don't we, as library managers, need Management Information System for libraries and information centers for decision making and efficient functioning? The answer is definitely yes and let us look into various aspects of Management Information System for library and information centers.

Library managers must have information concerning each aspect of their operations, functions and services. As a processor of information, a manager should collect, store, process, retrieve and utilize information required for decision making. Keeping abreast with all his requirements of information (both internal and external) in this ever expanding and complex library and information situation is beyond the capacity of individual library managers. As such a system has to be planned, designed and evolved to take care of this crucial information requirement of information people.

Definition and Meaning of Management Information System

There are numerous definitions of Management Information System. Yet the fundamental concept remains essentially the same. Management Information System can be defined as a collection of data processing equipment, procedures, software and people that integrates the sub-systems of the organization and provides information for decision making on planning and control operations. In other words, Management Information System is an integrated user-machine system that monitors and retrieves data from the environment, captures data from transactions and operations within the firm, filters, organizes and selects data and presents them as information to managers, and also provides the means for managers to generate information as desired. In simple terms Management Information System is any organized approach for obtaining relevant and timely information on which to base management decisions.

Historically, accounting systems provide information for planning and control in business. Managers have always had sources of information. But Management

Information System, with computerized processing of data provides a comprehensive system of information. Management Information System is a powerful method for aiding managers in operations analysis for solving problems and making decisions.

REVIEW QUESTIONS

1. Discuss the principles of management.
2. Write briefly on the functions of administration.
3. Examine the levels of management.
4. Examine the Management Information System.

2

Management of Routine Works of LIC's

LEARNING OBJECTIVE

After studying this unit, you will be able to:

- Know the LICs bodies of library
- Discuss the reports of the library.
- Know the organizational structure in libraries.

Introduction

In 1960 some libraries and data centres in India tried in a pair of second generation general computers available in Kanpur and Bombay to "automate" their library routines and data facilities. In 1964 the CEO of INSDOC led experiments in document and data work with computers to be used. Initially, the model used by IIT Kanpur was the IBM 1620 model I. The first try was to collect information for a scientific serial union directory.

In order to achieve better customer satisfaction the application of IT in libraries required fresh types of library services. After IT was implemented in libraries and data centres, the digital library service developed. IT has had a major effect and the features of data services produced in libraries have effectively altered. Due to information technology, the last two decades saw huge changes in the library. The technological progress has had an important effect on knowledge development and the unlocking of human potential. The effects on data resources, services and people are obviously apparent in the library.

2.1. Acquisition, Technical Processing, Circulation, Serial Control Acquisition

Acquisition is one of every library's significant tasks. The objective of a library to fulfil customers demand only to be met by the library procurement scheme, i.e. if the user acquires research materials based on his requirements then only he will be truly satisfied. This will apply to both modern and old libraries. The lending also leads to efficient and effective library collection growth, and therefore the acquisition of library materials is a significant task and also extremely labour intensive. Automation in this field is therefore very necessary.

The major objectives of an automated acquisition system may be:

1. Removal of the multiple manual files that take a lot of time from the personnel who internally remove errors of reporting, control, etc.
2. Improve precision in every aspect of the procurement process.
3. More efficient and effective treatment of cancellations and claims.
4. Financial records, accounting and reporting are more precise and timely.
5. Remove the need for manual discount processing.

Foreign exchange and other invoice data.

6. Enhanced tracking methods for orders, receipts and invoices.
7. Improved binding controls, including binding information records maintenance, alert delivery, binding order manufacturing, and monitoring.
8. Cataloguing integration and serial control for more efficient bibliographical holdings.
9. Providing the information required for management.
10. Enhances user services by fast, time-consuming order and receipt processing.

Technical Processing

Technical processing implies technical library services and library collection maintenance operations. Technical Services are the backdrop of operations undertaken by the library to process publicly loaned library material. Most of the functions of technical services are related to ordering, reclamation and receipt of material; cataloguing, material classification and serial control. Other technical services include the purchase and repair and conservation of material from libraries.

Progress in ICT is made, and libraries move towards an automated library system. Library automation enables librarians and other personnel in technical processing fields such as purchases, classification, cataloguing and distribution, etc. Automated cataloguing requirements such as MARC enable library personnel to readily list library objects. MARC (Machine Readable Cataloguing)

Library Automation facilitates the finding of books, the buying of the book, access to publications and books from the computer online. Automation can also assist to remove from the collection and strength library precious books ancient, out-of-date and meaningless books and equipment. Online classification tools like OCLC assist very easily with classification of library products.

Acquisition of library implies the acquisition of library material. The collection development policy and the choice of library materials are accepted as a first step in library acquisitions. Library is an organism that growing fast. The primary goals of the purchase of libraries are therefore to meet the user by supplying informative data. The acquisition of library material comprises the selection, purchase and organisation.

A classification of the library is a system for code, organization and the assign of a call number to this information resource and for document or library materials according to their subject matter. In libraries, classification schemes usually have two roles. First, by enabling the reader to find out what works or records the library has on a given topic, they promote topic access. Secondly, the data source is situated in a known place. If the material is organized in a library based on variables other than subjects, the arrangement will not meet the demands of most readers who generally approach a library for topics. Documents should, in other words, be categorized and arranged according to their topic material. The Academic Library is currently using the other institute's DDC (Various Editions), OCLC, Union Catalogue and Web OPAC as call numbers. Library catalogues are restricted to a single library or group of libraries, but today almost every library catalogue has the same fundamental search and organizational characteristics. In the 1970s, the online catalogues became almost obsolete, but for decorative or commemorative purposes certain libraries retained card catalogues. For the cataloguing of library files the library uses AACR normative cataloguing principles and CCC normative cataloguing principles. I would like to examine how the catalogue was published by the book, the public publishing entry and the records of the meeting.

Traditionally, the technical departments have performed those duties related to the transfer and getting of materials into the library. Public services have managed operations which have been directly used by end users in the collection of libraries and other collections to obtain access to data.

The catalogue of the library is regarded to reflect the book's collection, that is, whether the library has the right, the wrong or the right collection. It is regarded the basis for most operations of the library such as purchase, reference, inter-library loans and so on. The catalogue is referred to during purchasing activities to ensure that reading materials do not duplicate. The catalogue is consulted for reference and inter-library credit operations and other records which can be supplied on the loan or consulted to provide answers to reference questions. The catalogue is therefore seen in the library as a significant instrument. Therefore, if catalogue automation is achieved, the customers and employees benefit greatly from the fact that they can get the data they want without time. Similarly, if the catalogue is accessible via LAN in a network setting, users can access the same database at the same time. The library personnel will also enjoy the automated system because it eliminates their print work for cards, submits cards, and updates the catalogue and so on. In contrast to the big catalogue cabinet, which has a lot of room in the library, the automated catalogue also retains room.

Printed Index

Computers were used to prepare in-house indexes within the library, for the collection of information, and also to produce indexes for the most important abstract journals. The index comprises of a number of alphabetical terms. There are various kinds of indexes generated by computer:

KWIC (Key Word in Context)

An entry for a document is given in the document's name in a KWIC type index with each keyword. The computer has to be told how keywords are derived these are the words that distinguish the topic.

KWOC (Key word Out of Context)

The keyword is still in the name in this index. This technique raises the index size considerably, but if many entries are in one word, they divide the entries accordingly. It is used to index reports, publications, patents, etc. by several specialized libraries.

PRECIS (Preserved Context Index System)

In any important word, the user can enter an alphabetical topic code that together constitutes a compound declaration and then sets the whole context in which the author has taken into account the term selected.

POPSI (Postulate Based Permuted Subject Indexing)

This index is determined by word order and related symbols. The seating, postulated categories or relational operators define and define the order of words components within the chain.

Selective Dissemination of Information (SDI)

In SDI the data provided in a library corresponds to the users ' subjects; therefore the user only gets those data that are applicable to the study job he undertakes. A user profile is established in the computerized SDI system. At the same time, when papers are obtained in the library, the document profile will also be established. Both profiles are matched and sent to the user by the computer. The user receives feedback. Should the customer not be satisfied, the profiles are inspected and adapted according to the assessment of the user.

Reference Service

Initially, the reference librarian's relayed to perform the search and reply to factual or bibliographical questions on printed indexing and abstracting services, bibliographical sources and directories. Today however, it is clear that important reference books such as encyclopaedias, directories, bibliographies are either available as CD-ROMs or on the internet in the non-print format. They can be used as a database to access query reply data.

Circulation

The key element of a traffic control system is documents transaction, i.e. issuance and return. This database includes bibliographic data on papers containing data about titles, writers and data on publication that can be used to report the overdue to the customers. It includes loading and unloading library materials, reservations, statistics, sending reminders of overdue material, etc.

Automated circulation control features:

1. Information about circulation items place.
2. Listing of credit products to a certain borrower or borrowers' class.
3. Registration of holding or private reserves for credit products but often with a supplementary clause to notify library employees when the item is returned and printed a' book notification accessible' to e-mail to the people who requested it.
4. Notices for long-term credit products for printing recall.
5. Lending renewal.
6. Bibliography personnel notification of overdue products and overdue notice printing.
7. Notification at the moment of a requested credit or at the moment when the creditor leaves the organization or on demand forms the library of diligent creditors (i.e. those with unpaid penalties or overdue books).

8. Fines calculated, fine notices printed, fines recorded and fine receipt printable at times.
9. Statistics of different kinds are calculated and printed.
10. Summary statistics and statistics on the movement of specific products for procurement, service planning, and other administrative purposes are analyzed both.
11. Provision for the printing of due date files, the automatic generation of book orders lost, or the printing of mailing labels for remote borrowers.

Serial Control

Serials are released at periodic intervals and are to be published permanently. The word serial control generally refers to two very different elements: bibliographical control and processing control, apart from academic journals and famous periodicals: magazines and all other periodical publishing's, such as newsletters, newspapers, and annual reports, the procedures of learned entities, Monographs, etc. The control of the bibliographic serials includes preparing and maintaining a central master list of all serial publications, including full title, short titles, early change forms, publishers, ISSN, frequency etc. Control of serials includes procurement, checks on claims, cataloguing, circulation, binding, weeding out and so on.

Problems in Serials Control

Serial management is component and parcel of the activities of the library. It has fewer titles in comparison with the procurement scheme, but it has to record more information on each title and is therefore one of the most complicated and costly processes.

The following serial control issues

1. On a specific date not all publishers publish periodicals.

2. The publishing frequency can alter.
3. A change of title may occur.
4. They are sent by mail, air lift, air mail or sear-mail, and the shipping times and misplacement of these schemes have their own issues.
5. Foreign newspapers take about 10-15 weeks, but air mail is more expensive to achieve the target.

Serial control means those tasks involving serial acquisition and management in a library.

The Functions of Serials Control

An automated serial control system has features of the following:

1. Enter the information for problems in the library.
2. Order fresh serials and renovate the newspapers currently subscribed.
3. Recalls monitoring missing questions. Send them.
4. Accession by the library of individual problems.
5. Cancelation of newspapers currently subscribed.
6. Budget control for the binding subscription etc.
7. Problem binding when a given amount has been completed.

2.2. STOCK VERIFICATION

Stock check or physical checking is to verify and account for papers obtained by the library on a periodic basis. In terms of educators, scientists and library professionals, stock check is an irrelevant element of libertarianism. In reality, however, inventory checks are regarded to be a delicate, contentious and undesirable bad business. Learning librarians are often disturbed and concerned about the checking method and its consequences and outcomes. When books are subject to inventory testing, the mind and philosophy of libertarianism to books as animate humans full of emotion dissipate. In this respect, some see inventory checks as one of the job risks. The remaining dangers include document mutilation and loss of supply in transit. Stock checks are often carried out like a ritual, without clearly identifying goals and objectives and therefore a lot of confusion surrounds inventory checks. The process is simple and straightforward if the purposes and procedures of physical verification and responsibility for documents loss are clearly listed.

Stock Verification: Purpose

The price of conducting an inventory check often goes far beyond the advantages obtained and even the losses found, especially in a vibrant, extensive, well-structured and compact collection like that of a unique Library. There are, therefore, no beneficial advantages at the beginning of this post-mortem or pointless practice, other than account for the inventory. This can, however, cause users inconvenience, trouble library routines, and health hazards for library personnel, loss of man hours, time, and money and library services. The parent organization and the regulations governing it are mostly decided whether to take up such an activity or not when taken up at what frequency and whether it is for the entire collection, a sampling gathering etc. For instance, in respect of the government of India (1983,1984) organizations1 a library with no more than 20,000 volumes and no less than two skilled employees is to perform a full annual physical book verification. Factory libraries with up to 20 000 volumes with only one skilled library employees, as well as libraries that have more than 20000 volumes but have not more than 50,000 volumes must be physically verified at intervals of not more than 3 years. Moreover, in cases in which libraries have more than 50,000 volumes, we only need a sample physical test in intervals not exceeding 5 years. If uncommon or unreasonable shortages occurred during such sample verification, full verification shall be performed. Which sort of document is necessary to count for this purpose, but books and bound volumes of publications that ignore ephemeral and gray literature and microforms can be presumed to be included.

Advantages of Stock Veritification

Some benefits should also be noted by a library when conducting inventory checks. First, the regular inventory checks and write-offs of resulting losses contribute to reducing unnecessary book value escalations of assets. Second, physical checking also helps replace appropriate, helpful and requested records with fresh copies, wherever they are lost or mutilated. Thirdly, it's time to implement fresh methods of stack arrangement, altered or fresh lending systems and other processes in inventory verification. Fourthly, when a library calls back all records provided for inventory checks it can give its users the chance, after verification, to browse the whole collection. This contradicts the otherwise less valuable books which lie on racks all year round. Fifthly, the inventory check enables review the precautionary steps that have already been taken to prevent loss and mutilation and to recognize any deficiencies in the current library and vigilance maintenance procedure. In particular, inventory check helps to detect and discard out-dated quantities. The loss of on demand books is usually observed only in a day-to-day working time in an active collection of a well-organized library. Additional incidental advantages of inventory checks include identification of damaged, used repair or rewinding documents, maintaining the inventory list and other up-to-date records as well as rearranging and cleaning stacks, making library employees more familiar with collection and documents, and so on.

Methods of Stock Verification

The parent organization may, or may not involve

internal individuals in the stock checking team as regards procedures for carrying out inventory checks and may decide to exclude certain kinds of content from the library. The rest of the verification methodology depends on the provisions already drawn up on library record design and organization. For inventory verification, several techniques are followed. The crudest technique is to count the amount of files in numerical numbers and practically does not work except to understand how many files have been lost. The ancient and relatively crude technique is to verify and ecord records on accession register racks physically. Not only does this technique take time and time but the entire register must also be retained during the checking process. It can also result in ticking marks spoiling the register. However, the initial register could still be saved with the introduction of fresh reproduction methods of the accession register. A further system that also has the disadvantage of maintaining the complete register (or substitute) is that cards containing registration numbers are printed, pre-written, written and printed in blocks of 100 digits, while the papers are physically checked on racks. The simultaneous operation of the number of bats in the two methods depends on the number of copies of the accession register or its substitute available and the results of the control from various copies / batches have to be reassessed if more than one copy of the accession registry is used. All these make it not only lourd, but also waste time and effort. With the proliferation of private computers, it is also feasible to enter all accession figures only if the loss in terms of the missing accession numbers is checked and consolidated. The cheapest and quickest way to enter the accession number consists of scanning book accession numbers from the bar code in the books with a portable bar code / wall-reader. However, in this nation, there is still a bar code scheme to collect. The basic, relatively trustworthy and fast manual technique for checking inventory is the shelf list. This procedure needs an updated shelf list. The closing library for verification is required by all this techniques. Another technique based on shelf lists that do not require a library to be shut down, but guarantees that two (book) card schemes are fairly cost effective, fast, and reliable inventory insurance. For each document, two distinct colour cards are prepared and one of them is kept as a shelf list card and the other as a book. The two book cards will be exchanged at the moment of the inventory check. This technique enables many batches to operate simultaneously, as both the shelf list and records are arranged in the same sequence and enable the correction of inventory checking mistakes at a subsequent date.

For stock verification there are three methods.

They are:

(i) Stock verification periodically.

(ii) Stock verification perpetually.

(iii) Stock taking blindly.

(i) Periodic verification : This approach covers the entire inventory at the end of a financial year at the same moment. Only in a small scale organization can this be achieved. However, this approach does not fit large scale organizations, since it is not only possible to stop job for several days for stock-taking purposes.

(ii) Perpetual verification : According to this procedure, physical stock control is conducted throughout the year under a default program. And every product at least once a year is physically examined.

Advantages : Four major benefits of perpetual verification are:

(i) Neither shops nor works shall be shut down during the physical check.

(ii) The transaction and posting of ordinary shops may proceed without interruption.

(iii) Occasionally surpluses and scarcity may be written-off after adequate inquiry.

(iv) The inventory check can be performed on a timely basis.

(iii) Blind verification : The position will be given to the inventory checkers, but no code numbers, description and inventory record balance information is provided in this system. The fundamental logic here is that without a real verification of its inventory the checker will not have his own idea about the inventory positions.

This is not a common procedure. When the entire operation of the shops is well planned, it serves nearly no end. The contemporary trend is to apply the ABC inventory verification method.

Who Should Do The Stock Taking?

Owners are needed to store their own stocks in some of the organizations. This is not the right thing to do. It not only causes them to hide true differences in order to prevent sanctions, it also contributes to intentional looting or fraud in cases of surplus.

It's the straightforwardness of things to hire full-time auditors to perform this task. They can however use the support of warehouses and even engineering personnel to identify themselves correctly.

Treatment of Discrepancies (Reconciliation)

Stock quantities discovered in the physical exam are often not consistent with inventory records. There are therefore some differences. There is a surplus where the inventory is more than that, and where there is a shortage in it.

Surpluses : Surpluses arise for the following three reasons:

(a) Where the bins don't produce products, but issue shall be entered.

(b) Where there is less than the quantity for which an

entry is made, where the quantity of material is issued.

(c) Where there is only the item entry is made in the inventory.

Shortages : Shortage may occur for the following six reasons:

(a) Excessive physical issues than real issue entries.

(b) Issues created, but not in the issue column, matching entries.

(c) The excess amount for which the entries in the issue column are produced is exceeded.

(d) Issue without requirement of materials.

(e) Mistreatment.

(f) Materials are defective.

Importance of Stock Verification

Many libraries performed inventory checks for losses and count their collection. Regular inventories show that reform can be implemented through weakness and strength in the process. Stock control can help you understand, keep, and arrange the asset; delete or replace lost items; and give the user adequate facilities. The current research aims to study the collection protection inventory verification carried out in university library. For example inventory verification or asset check, physical checks on books on shelf and maintaining books from harm outside their places. These are distinct types of inventory verification. The loss of books and materials, missing books, keeping damaged books by binding, the repair of machinery or buildings, etc., and preventing precious property in libraries is helped by such stocks or audits.

To know the stock pattern technique and frequency of college libraries. To ensure its collection, each library should perform regular inventory checks. The library holdings must be updated to record the loss ratio.

To understand how libraries are used as a shelf list, accession register or number, dummy Book Card to manual library locations. Stock check helps keep check on files, shelf, fixes bugs, organize the shelf list, locate missing items, etc. It helps to update the existing catalogue of books according to the inventory and products withdrawn.

Precautionary Measures Against Loss

The very first issue to be asked after the inventory inspections in a library is,' are current safeguards against the loss of papers in the library sufficient? And' is it possible to take any additional precautions? (This might even be one of the inventory check goals). Preventive and precautionary measures here again usually cost much more than their value. The common precautions used when planning a library are for one entry from a exit to the library, so that personal belongings are prevented from passing through the windows and cover all windows of the building with appropriate cable meshes or metal grill. Other precautions, including a security guard, a magnet document control / alarm and other electronic safety system, CCTV, a loss insurance company etc. include a check point at the exit door and a vigilance workplace, cost the organization significantly in relation to not being foolish evidence. What further precautions are taken depend on how much more expensive the organization is prepared to incur (i.e. in excess of the price of inventory checks). There need to be unique mention of two stuffs here. First of all, some expenses such as wages are often unseen by surveillance workers. Secondly, every physical inspection by a safety guard in a reputable organization can not only provide users with resistance, but also a hideous display. In addition to intensifying vigilance, the liberalization of facilities such as longer library hours during examination time, the liberal or subsidized Xerox and the liberal lending of the marked' not to be given' is another beneficial strategy. It's natural to wonder how library books are lost in study establishments, where most consumers of library books are from greater classes. Mysteriously, no person or group of people can be identified. Such robberies are not simple to capture. Surprisingly, the legal procedure is so brittle where they are caught that it is hard to find a robbery. Bibliographers are not a police officer in any manner. In the course of the discussion about multiple safety techniques Pierce (1980p271-249) says, the preservation of safety of the material in the library has altered from a little irritant to a significant issue. Many libraries found they lose over 1% of their collections each year[and] vandalism; 2 The assessment of book kinds lost and the distribution of value of books lost should give instructions on books losing their need for vigilance, changes in arrangements, and the way they are organized. 2 Analyse of the kinds of books lost should give a few rules. It would be very valuable to analyse this with helpful ratios3 like usage losses, inventory losses (in value), losses per customer per year, etc. One such loss assessment for the 1987-88 ISRO Satellite Centre (ISAC) Library is provided in Annex I. He showed obviously that text books or other common works, which cost much less than the average price of books obtained, are lost in office regulations, electronics, computer science, etc. A ratio analysis of ISAC Library losses is provided in Annex II. Annex II shows that for each Rupee in inventory Re 0.0005 is lost in one year and 0.0458 (or 4 records per 100 customers per year) or Rs. 3.09 worth papers are lost in one year for every User. Documentation is lost. In addition, on average 3.67 papers per 1000 files in inventory are lost. As for Govt. ISAC Library lost just 0.58 documents from India guideline (previously mentioned) to allow 3 books for each 1000 published / consulted. Finally, the ISAC library loss is only 80% of the by-products in the form of nominal overdue library fees.

Despite liberalized facilities and rigorous vigils, a

negligible amount of perverted, possessive, accustomed individuals accountable for loss and mutilation are likely to continue. Furthermore, the competent agency needs to explain and write-off what has already been lost and what will be detected in future inventory verifications. At this point it is often indirectly a case of librarian or librarian and his employees to ask who is to take responsibility for the loss of library records, although most special libraries and data centres are managed directly or indirectly by non-librarians either as boards or as agent accountable. The librarian can be held directly accountable for the loss in certain libraries. Loss of moving property, shopping and consumer goods is a universal phenomenon. The loss of various kinds of moveable estate, shops and consumables is incurred for individuals, institutes, departments, government and private companies. An individual library user who releases a book taken out of the library pays the replacement costs to the library has the right and vengeful feeling to do what is lost by the librarian. However, he forgets to differentiate librarian from librarian as a functional library head as an individual user. There is so much fusion over loss accountability in none other field of loss such as those of minor machinery and consumables within any organization as it occurs in the loss of library records. As an instrument to punish librarians, this inventory check is covertly regarded. Librarian provides services to customers by opposing the loser of files deposited in his name and by recovering the' replacement costs' of files he is receiving a psychological dislike or hate. In an organization, recoveries are rarely made for the loss of smaller equipment and consumables even though they have been issued for the exclusive ownership of individuals. The loss of library records is small, compared with the magnitude of losses for many different shop products in an organization. Secondly, products in shops, including smaller equipment, were exclusively held under lock and key and no need to be shared. In fact, books published to each department are often lost. In addition, all other kinds of articles with door passes are subject to rigorous safety. Documents in the open access library, on the other hand, are intended for many people to share. Library personnel are not intended to maintain library custody on their own. Comparing the loss of library materials with the loss of store articles demonstrates obviously that losses of libraries are inevitable. For reasons of reasoning, a library may use an anti-service approach and advocate a door pass scheme that protects a closed access library. But the essence of library services is being removed. In order to impose constraints, the results of inventory verification should not be applied. In any organization, where librarians and their colleagues are fully accountable for the document losses and for the loss of their salary, it is clear that, in line with the benefits given to jobs like that of a cashier at offices, he and his colleagues who share the responsibility are given a' risk benefit' as well as free modification of the library. However, if the scenario is not justifiable for librarians and librarians to inquire into negligence and reject duty, the more sensible way of resolving the impasse of liability is to treat the loss of library records as any other loss in an institution and write-off by the competent authority. The laws governing the organization would show the economic powers and the scope of losses permitted for write-offs. If it is Government. For instance, In the rank not below that of the Deputy Secretary to the Government, Indian institutions (as referenced above) librarian The loss of library records to the extent of economic powers and monitoring constraints may occur from India or the Head of the Department with economic powers. A loss of three volumes for each 1000 volumes published / consulted in one year shall be suggested as an acceptable loss limit unless the loss has been attributed to the librarian's dishonesty or negligence. Invariable loss of the Rs.200/-* book and the books of unique nature and scarcity and consequential actions shall be explored. Further rare unique books and books may be held under shutdown. The above guidelines also stipulated that no objection should be raised as long as they are based on the suggestions of a three member panel appointed by the Department for the disposal of mutilated / damaged / outdate materials to the best interests of the library. Many officials have, in practice, a special way to examine fresh policies, processes and facilities, including the deletion of losses.

Verification of library stocks is not only an unnecessary evil that benefits customers and library personnel very little but has some benefits. Depending on the organization of documents, the scale of job and the accessibility of instruments and people, many ways can be completed rapidly and efficiently. Depending on the institution's bag there are a range of cautionary measures to prevent the loss of library documents. However, the costs of such initiatives often far outweigh the savings the library can offer. A work hazard for libertarianism arose from the problem of fixing responsibilities for loss of library records. Rationalizing and updating guidelines for inventory checks and limitations on write-offs for losses in service focused libraries would take far to provide customers with better facilities. Particularly the instructions on the type of material (i.e. books and bound newspapers only) to be covered for inventory verification should be made more specific and rational about setting the book price threshold for start-up enquiry and intervention. It might be reasonable to say that a book that costs more than 150 percentage of the average cost of the book that is purchased during the year should only be further investigated when it is lost. In this respect, professional bodies play an essential role.

2.3. LIBRARY RECORDS

Libraries retain various kinds of documents to monitor their routine tasks according to defined standards. In the course of library operations and services, some data is generated and stored before the library becomes operational. As a bibliography student, in the context of the library you have to understand and learn about the nature and type of such records and their functions. In this Unit we will study library records, their significance, their requirements, types and the roles documents play in different library segments.

In the course of their business, records are established and captured by people or organizations. Most documents are evidence of operations linked to administration, management, service or work. Literature, minutes, memoranda, accounts etc. are traditional records. Data sheets, databases, e-mails and telecopies are included in the electronic log formats. What technology has done in certain respects is to redefine traditional formats of documents. E-mail is very much like a letter, for instance. It is that the e-mail distinguishes from letters is transferred electronically.

The registers provide data in the form of an organization or an organization's descriptions, stats or activities. Not all sources of data are necessarily records when all documents transmit data. For instance, no record is made online or offline with a published book or an externally supplied database, but it could itself be recorded by selecting Andre-using data in a fresh context.

The transaction records continue to accumulate, and when the activity is completed, the records are in the form of documents with full history, process and outcome. The exercise can be a policy, a transaction or the establishment of a new service. Records are viewed in this sense as an instant picture of an action or event. They're giving an image of what occurred.

Current events produce records. For example, a rare book exhibition would generate a number of records from questions that visitors can put to the exhibition managers, and also from the views that they can record on an exhibition in the visitor's book prior to their departure. Records which may emerge from this type of case would include: some documents, a booklet, a bibliography of the books displayed, the book of tourists, etc.

Some records are used in both current and future applications, while others must be used as source material only in the future. For example, when another exhibition is being held, files created for the exhibition will be used mainly in the future. On the other hand, both now and in the future the bibliography of books can be used.

For a long time, the word record is used in archives. However, it is now commonly used in industries, organizations, organizations and libraries. In library science, it relates to papers that contain information of the processes, activity and outcomes of the whole or part of the organization.

ISO 15489: International Record Management Standard describes a registration as: "recorded information in any way, including data on a computer system, produced, obtained and retained in the course of company transactions as proof and data of an organization or of a individual."

A library is an organization that obtains, processes, and provides the clientele with data sources in its multiple forms, such as books, serials, microfiches, CDs, etc. libraries also produce many documents, both in descriptive form and in the form of statistical tables, by providing funds and then providing multiple services.

Need For Records

The documents contain data that demonstrate the tasks carried out and operations carried out and thus provide an important source of understanding of how and why choices are taken. Given the valuable documents for any organization, they must be properly created and managed to guarantee present and future responsibility and to promote future activities. The necessity for properly managing records is also demonstrated by the critical role that records play in protecting the interests of the library during periods of crisis and in fulfilling the official audits, investigations and reviews by external agencies. We are able to understand that for a number of reasons, library needs records: records are necessary for recording actions and decisions taken in the library and for the orderly, efficient and accountable conduct of library business.

Records are needed for the management and administration of libraries to be consistent, continuous and productive.

- Records are required to provide services in a coherent and fair way, as records contribute to the harmonization and maintenance of routines.
- To support and document policy and management decision-making and encourage informed decision-making, all the records are required.
- Benchmark measures are provided in the records to track and assess progress in performance, effectiveness and performance.
- Records provide assistance for policy development and revision, programs, systems and strategic plans for the long term.
- Records support different library proposals, including building development as well as demand for extra employees, as well as suggestions for extra funding for acquisitions, new services and services, etc.
- Catalogue Records serves as an effective instrument for accessing library resources. Records are available.

- Records as evidence of budget use to meet audit demands. Records
- Major records of aid to rational employee distribution across different departments.
- Background records as data on the use of services to justify parent management and society library expenses.

Types of Library Records

Unlike registers of government or industrial buildings, most of which are files, library accounts are created and captured in various forms depending on the nature of the activities in various departments of the library. The corresponding software modules generate such documents in a completely computerized library. The dominant types of documents are ledgers, registers, files, cards and statistical sheets in non-automated libraries.

Records may be categorised according to

(i) Their lives,

(ii) Their content and

(iii) How the data are presented.

(i) Records as per their Life Span : These records are categorised as :

(i) Permanent,

(ii) Semi-permanent, and

(iii) Temporary.

Permanent Records **:** Documents that will be permanently maintained include documentation on the library policy, library processes, and policy guidelines, library origin and development documents, approvals to employees, membership registers, user registration forms, audit reports, furniture inventory, fitting and equipment, a construction plan, electrical and sewage systems plans, etc.

Semi-permanent Records **:** Among other things, these documents include the Use Register, contracts with companies regarding book supply terms and conditions, access to databases and library circulation documents, in-house documents and internet usage documents. Until the audit is finished, financial reports are kept. Likewise, documents concerning the terms and conditions of supply of a company must not be kept once the company has been dealt with.

Temporary Records **:** Records produced for a particular job must be demolished when the work is finished. For instance, when the books are catalogued, book selection cards / slips are generally demolished. In cases of being used as an accession record, these are not demolished. Also a temporary record is a serial enrolment card. After it's complete, a fresh card will replace it.

(ii) Records as per their Content : These records include:

(i) Service records,

(ii) Financial records,

(iii) Administrative records and

(iv) Records of resources

Records of Resources **:** These documents are for audio, audio-visually, computer, brochures, theses, globes, maps, microfiches, microfilms, pictures, postcards, posters, reports, serials, photographs and stamps. These documents include audio and non-book materials.

Financial Records **:** Financial records include books of accounts such as the budget register and sectional funds allotment registers as well as the bill registry. Library Service Records–These records include inter-library loan records and circulation records, etc.

Administrative Records **:** The amount of employees differs between libraries and libraries. There are libraries run by only one employee. Others have employees ranging between a few and over 100. Each employee has a service document, which keeps records of his entire service from his service request. Also closely maintained are confidential reports of all employees written by their elders. All these administrative documents are essential.

(iii) Records by Form of Presentation : These documents are descriptive and statistical in two different kinds. Descriptive documents are the annual reports of a library, the policies for the library, minutes of different conferences, etc.. In a year, a library buys, procedures and transmits books and to the readers. After they are sent back, they are replaced. There are several readers every day who use the library, some ask questions, want certain services, etc. At year-end, cumulative data will be analysed and the data generated indicating the number of books purchased, processed, issued, number of queries replied to and photocopies provided, etc. Those are records of statistics.

Records Maintained by the Individual Sections of Libraries

Libraries under a departmental framework organize their operations. The real design of a library's organizing structure relies on its size, the length of its library tasks or its administrative requirements. In libraries the following structure is more prevalent with marginal differences

(i) Acquisition Section

(ii) Reference and Documentation Service Section

(iii) Circulation-cum-Reading Room Section

(iv) Technical Processing Section

(v) Periodicals Section

(vi) Administration Section

(vii) Maintenance Section

Each section creates and maintains records to help conduct its routines in a systematic order.

Library terminology records contain detailed information about the procedures, operations and outcomes of certain tasks of the whole or portion of the organization. Records provide consistency in library duties and serve as a standard for performance assessment. The papers for fresh suggestions are used as supporting documents and serve to compile the library history. They also contribute to the auditing of libraries and justify the need for a social organization. Records can be split into separate classifications using distinct criteria, such as life span, content and data presentation. Library records are kept as books, registers, cards / slips, and files.

2.4. ANNUAL RECORDS

Department / unit management generally assigns a individual to monitor and to guarantee that the entire department / unit carries out and completes the annual purge. The individual assigning this position could also be the formal Records Coordinator for a retention area / sub-area in which event the individual would play the role as described above. However, not all people entrusted with the annual purge of their own documents are also an official Records Coordinator.

The Report

- Report is an assessed outcome that contains particular contents covering all data relating to the particular subject.
- Public or private reports may be public or oral, or written.
- Foreign, commercial and educational reporting shall be used.

Annual Report

- An annual report is an overview of the operations of a company during the previous year.
- The objective of the Annual Reports shall be to

provide data about the operations and economic results of the company to investors and other concerned parties.

Annual Report of Library

- The library's annual report reflects the job performed in the library during the last twelve months.
- The library's annual report summarizes the multiple library departments ' operations and achievements.

Objectives of Annual Report in Library

- To Display Library Service.
- Inform the library agency of the library's work.
- Keep track of the library's achievement and growth.
- Encourage donations, donations, and library donations to individuals, institutions, and society.
- Comparison with knowledge of the latest accomplishments of the prior annual report.
- Aid for library auditing.

Content of Annual Report in Library

- A brief history of library.
- Library authority and his functioning in previous year.
- Description of previous and recent services.
- Users of library.
- Collection of library.
- Library finance.
- Extension activities.
- Library staff.
- Other activities.

How to Prepare Annual Report for a Library

It is anticipated that any organisation will present its annual report. The Annual Library Report is the survey of the past year's job. The work and accomplishments of the library are summarised. This is a form of librarian reporting to greater levels of government.

The study of the real job performed in the previous year is an annual report. An annual shows the accessions and processing's of books, the services rendered, the introduction of fresh staff or facilities, the use of economic and other funds, performance evaluation and so on.

Purpose of the Annual Report

1. To learn about the actual economic situation and other aspects of the library's facilities from our board of trustees and other administrative officials.
2. To serve as an advertising media for consumeı s.
3. Helps compare annual accounts of several years that allow the librarian to determine the library's strengths and weaknesses. This helps him upgrade the library.
4. The location of the personnel can be checked and employees can be allocated in the library.
5. Access to the real requirements and find out how more resources are supplied.

Contents of Annual Reports

The most important feature of a report is its contents. A report may include the following main heads.

1. Area/Population served : In terms of provision of books and no book material per person of the population, the area or population served shows the scales of the library's services.

2. Stocks of books and non-book materials : Book inventories and non-book documents, such as images, prints, hand-outs, slides, phone-records, etc. In addition to the nature of the books and non-books as mentioned in the annual report, including the areas of expertise will assist the library to access its resources and to respond to its multiple requirements. At the beginning of the report year, the report shall show the total volumes on stock, the number of withdrawn volumes, the number of volumes added over the years, as well as the total number of volumes at end of year. Moreover, there must be a notice for the reader of the amount of present periodicals subscribed to.

3. Services (Technical and Readers service) : Technical services include classification, cataloguing, paperwork, reader services, photo reproductions, etc. The annual report shall indicate what classification scheme is followed, whether the catalogue services are in their physical and internal form and whether the employees are insufficient or not, as indicated in their annual report.

Technical operations such as indexing, abstraction and paperwork should be referenced and assessed as far as possible in special libraries. A statistical table can be attached to indicate the amount of topic books and their per-capita circulation etc.

The consultation service of Reader is the main element of modern library service. Proper statistics are essential in order for the description of such facilities to be included in the Annual Report to encourage the authorities to fund better facilities with the recent equipment and enhanced reference resources.

4. Clientele : The amount and the statistics indicating the proportion of people reader to be obviously displayed are registered readers, adults, kids, blind etc. Client statistics and their lecturing concerns will allow the librarian to assess the usefulness of a library as shown in circulation statistics.

5. Finance : In order to detect if the budget distribution is sufficient and needs to be increase, a library's current economic situation must be indicated in its annual report. Govt. revenue sources. It is necessary to display the fund, the Library Authority Fund, membership charges, fines from other sources and the complete revenue. The annual report shows all the spending on employees ' wages, books, and non-book materials, periodicals, equipment, heating, cooling, lighting, cleaning, etc., and overall expenses.

6. Staff : The number of staff,

The number of librarians and assistants

Clark and Typists

Caretakers, Sorters and Janitors

Cleaner

Binders and the total number of staff should be shown in the annual report.

7. Miscellaneous : Each year the annual report must contain activities such as extension services (readings, films, training programmes, seminars, conferences, study circle) and other events related to social and adult learning.

REVIEW QUESTIONS

1. Discuss in detail of Library Information Center.
2. Write briefly on the organizational structure in libraries.
3. Discuss in detail about Stock verification.
4. Discuss in detail about Annual Reports of Library.

3

Human Resource Management

LEARNING OBJECTIVES

After studying this unit, you will be able to:

- Know the Human Resource Management policy and staffing
- Discuss the role of Human Resource Development professionals in training.

3.1. INTRODUCTION OF HUMAN RESOURCE MANAGEMENT

The management of human resources (HRM) makes the best possible use of people to achieve their organizational goals. In the late 20th century, the concept was created; subsequently motivation and worker satisfaction came under focus rather than merely reasonable management (Hartel, Fujimoto, Strybosh and Fitzpatrick, 2007). The skills, creative talents and capabilities acquired in the population have been described as human resources. HRM focuses on the humanity dimension in leadership since it is important for every organization to consist of employees, to develop their expertise, to motivate them to achieve a high level of results and to continue to commit themselves to this organization to achieve their goals. This is irrespective of the sort of company–the government, company, etc. Academic library human resources management defined as "those procedures that are planned and implemented to build an efficient human resources system and to support all organizational aims."

Human Resource Planning

Human resources planning are an organization's most significant management function.

- It guarantees the appropriate provision of human resources.
- It guarantees good human resource quality.
- It guarantees efficient human resource usage.

(i) In light of organizational objectives, human resource planning shall include the human resource requirements.

(ii) Human resources planning needs to be focused on clear, well-defined goals.

(iii) The human resources plan must ensure that at the right time it does a job for which it is economically most suitable; it has the right number of people and the appropriate type of people.

(iv) The principle of periodic revision of the new evolutions should be taken into account for the planning of human resources and an extension of the plan to cover changes during the long term.

(v) The planning of the human resources should pave the way for an effective process of motivation.

(vi) The planning of human resources must be kept sufficiently flexible to meet evolving organizational requirements.

Elements of Human Resource Planning

The diverse aspects of human resources planning are:-

(i) Quantitatively and qualitatively assess employee demands;

(ii) Recruitment and staff selection.

(iii) Induction and use.

(iv) Development of staff.

(v) The quality assurance of products and services, the main objective being to maintain customer satisfaction.

(vi) Total performance evaluation and adjustment.

Estimating Manpower Requirements

Library is an increasing company. With the increasing size of libraries and data and its complexities, it is very important to estimate the demands of the workforce for libraries and information centers. In relation to the fundamental background in a topic sector, every professional, in relation to library and data science skills, must also have a computer and communication background.

Support employees of most libraries and data centers, ranging from paralegals to administrative and clerical employees, have a broad variety of skilled employees. The first stage in the preparation of human resources is the estimation of the staff needs for both the present and the future, taking account of organizational goals and planned developments. The employee demands for big organizations have to be estimated using forecasting methods systematically. The top management will have to estimate the need and obtain data from the line managers for the actual needs in the various units. In smaller organizations, the top individual exercises his organization's expertise and prediction skills.

The personnel needs for the library and the information center must be estimated based on what is to be achieved over a period of time on the activities, programs, projects and goals. A specific stage of development is the quantitative evaluation of demands over three to five years. At the same time, methods such as job analysis, job description and work assessment have to evaluate the quality of the individuals involved.

In the wake of dramatic modifications taking place over the next several days in libraries and data centers, fresh facilities such as literature search with CD-ROM, databases, sales and marketing of library and data center products need to be introduced and planned. Education and economic growth are definitely connected. Based on the projections of skilled workers demands for a particular period, the planners will show the direction in which the education industry develops during the same period.

There cannot always be precise forecasts in the scheduling phase. It should be an ongoing method for monitoring and assessment to be efficient. A plan horizon will be the first step in the manpower planning process. The duration that the employee plan applies should be known. Then it should be evident about the particular business goals and strategies. On the basis of these estimates of demand and supply predictions, the strategy and techniques can be used for manpower.

Professionals should have the advantage over non-professionals in libraries and data centers. The current personnel should be motivated to attend seminars of learned societies in order to work efficiently at contemporary information centers.

Recruitment and Selection

Recruitment is primarily a method to find sources of employment and to take effective steps to contact these staff, which forms efficient staff. The recruitment process consists of five separate components:

(a) Recruitment policy;
(b) Recruitment organization;
(c) Labor requirements predictions;
(d) Manpower growth; and
(e) Technology for using those sources.

The selection method includes positioning effectively. Effective job analysis and difference recruitment and positioning are the basis for the selection method. The method of choice generally includes 7 steps.

(a) Recruitment policy
(b) Recruiting organization
(c) Forecast of manpower requirements
(d) Development of manpower sources, and
(e) Techniques for utilizing these sources.

The process of selection involves placement in effective positions. The selection process depends upon effective job analysis and differential recruitment and placement. The selection process involves usually seven steps.

(a) Preliminary screening of applications.
(b) Review of application forms
(c) Physical examination
(d) Checking references
(e) Psychological testing
(f) Interview and
(g) Internal promotion programs.

Induction and Development

Induction implies installation or initiation. The fresh recruit is mounted and launched into the team that makes up the organization's workforce. Induction is a method to present and explain the position of fresh employees in an organization. Induction is essential because the feeling of fresh staff over this period can impact how they feel about the organization, for several years to come. It generally starts from a guided tour of the construction, etc.

Once the worker has his orientation towards the organization, the employee's deployment is called the most appropriate place. The capacity, responsibility, team work capacity and other personal characteristics are key factors when employees are deployed. Unless the staffs are deployed cautiously, the organizations will face severe conflict issues.

Personnel Development

Libraries and Information Center in India operate under the control and monitoring of the staff policies and plans of parent organizations as part of multiple institutional complexes, such as R & D establishments, universities, government departments etc. The development of human resources for an organization must draw up a plan for getting the best out of its carefully chosen staff to accomplish the organizational goals, goals of development and growth.

The various personnel development programs are:-

(a) Performance Appraisal of staff;

(b) Training and Development;

(c) Changing perspectives and attitudes;

(d) Communication.

Ensuring Quality to Products and Services

Quality circles are tiny groups of staff who usually work together to agree on ways to improve quality, productivity and so on. In library and data centers, global norms are accessible for maintaining quality.

A standard for information exchange is ensured in India, for instance, using the CCF format for database building. In short, this helps us to provide quality networking service.

Overall Assessment of Performance and Fine Tuning

Not just a one-off workout is planning. It is a continuous attempt to assess its efficiency in the current method of execution. During the execution of a plan, modifications may occur owing to different issues not expected during the preparation of a plan. The plan may need to be modified in practice when implementing the plan.

The efficacy of the plan should therefore be evaluated periodically in terms of the results obtained. The strength and weakness of the plan are identified in that sort of assessment. It is necessary to revise the fragile part of the scheme. This kind of evaluation would enable the plan to be returned for achievement.

3.2. JOB ANALYSIS

Job Analysis is an essential instrument for any organization's Human Resources Management (HRM). In every organization including libraries, Human Resources Management (HRM) has a significant management position. Proper assessments of employment guarantee that staff co-operate systematically and understand their work and the company. Job assessment is the process by which distinct facts and data about a job can be systematically disclosed and also serves to make the right workflow and common rules and regulations between staff one of the finest processes. It defines definite abilities, expertise, abilities, responsibilities and tasks for a particular job. It is the basis for job and job descriptions. Job description indicates that the minimum qualifications for carrying on a work express data concerning a job assignment, duties, responsibilities and description of a work.

Description of Job Analysis

Before undertaking the work evaluation study, the work analyst attempts to classify the various positions in an organization or institution where a specific task is a work unit. The task of classifying and identifying important tasks and responsibilities is hard for the work analyst. The work analyst will usually seek the assistance of specific topic specialists in the field of educators, practitioners, incumbents, managers, managers, public officials, multiple stakeholders, etc. in selecting the multiple key elements of the work sector. The various tasks, responsibilities, tasks and skills necessary for carrying out these tasks are an instrument for data sources for job analysis. Job analysis therefore plays a key role in streamlining the work and achieving the objectives of an organization. The regular job analysis by a skilled job analyst helps the company to improve employee performance and services. The different ranges of data collected in the work evaluation process provide the officials and policymakers with a ready-to-use instrument which helps decision-makers and politicians, human resources planning, recruitment, selection, training and growth, performance evaluation, compensation and advantages, security, health and hygiene, and legal aspects. The results of this study immediately describe the job and specify the job.

In the assessment of the job there are many distinct definitions. These definitions are invented at various times by various academics and personalities. These definitions include two popular and significant terms: "Job assessment is about data about employment, in particular about what the working person does and does, why he does it, skills, preparation and education necessary, relationships with other employment, physical requirements, the environment, etc." and "the other" as follows According to Jean Jones and Thomas Decothis (1969).

Evaluation of Job Analysis

The only factor determining pay structures cannot

be a job evaluation because the assessment of jobs involves relationships, but is not absolute. It should be mentioned here. The methods used for the work assessment include ranking, classification, rating points, etc.

Job analysis offers different work data. Some significant data in the work evaluation is as follows.

(a) Identify the task and the job title.

(b) The specific operation and activities which make up a task and its relative timings and significance, the simplicity, the routine or the complexity of assignments, the responsibility for other persons, the assets or the resources, and what the typical employee does. (c) What the typical employee does;

(c) The work circumstances and the working environment.

(d) Metals, plastics, grains, yarns and lathes, frame machines, electronic ignition testers, maize huskers, punch presses and micrometers are illustrative of the products and equipment's that are in use by the working person.

(e) How the work is done: emphasis is put on the nature of the work and activities, including manipulation, feeding, removal, drilling, conduction, installation, and many other activities.

(f) The attributes of staff required: the experience, learning, physical strength, coordination, physical requirements, mental capacity, abilities and social skills.

(g) The working circumstances and the working environment shall contribute greatly to the work results and employee satisfaction.

Principles of job evaluation

There are some principles in the job evaluation. The work evaluators should keep these values in mind. These principles are not only guidelines for an adequate work assessment but also clarify the assessment process.

The following principles are, according to Kress:

1. Evaluate the work and the employer. Each component should be rated according to the task itself;
2. The components chosen for rating reasons should be readily explained in terms and a few in number and cover without overlapping the required requirements for each job;
3. Clear definition and correct selection of the components;
4. Every work rating plan has to be sold to counselors and staff. A clear explanation and an illustration of the plan will be the basis for the achievement of sales;
5. Foreman should be involved in job ratings in his own departments;
6. Employees can achieve maximum collaboration if they can discuss employment scores and;
7. There should not be too many occupational salaries. An employer's salary for each total of item values would be unwise.

Regular collection, recording and data about employment are very essential for the job analysis. This data is collected and evaluated by employers and officials on various occasions during the assessment. Furthermore, this data helps employers and the authorities to decide the quality and amount of services, responsibilities, operating environment etc.

The work evaluation plan method begins with the choice of the correct individual to be used to conduct the job analysis. In an organization the following three distinct categories of people or organizations usually conduct a work assessment:

(a) By a Temporary Job Analyst : A temporary work analyst can be hired from outside by the authority or organization to analyze work in its company.

(b) By Employing a Full Time Job Analyst : A full-time job analyst may be designated by the competent authority. Since the work assessment is an ongoing method, it enables much to keep the data about the work assessment properly recorded.

(c) By an Employer, Supervisor, Job Incumbent or a Combination of Both : Appointing supervisors, employees, or combinations of both supervisors and employees may perform a job analysis. It is usually practiced in organizations in the public industry.

Uses and Advantages of Job Analysis

Job analyzes are regarded an essential component for the management of staff. For all ranges of staff and the general human resource planning system such as recruitment, selection, training and growth, wage / salary management, work layout, performance evaluation, compensation and advantages, health, sanitation and security, legal issues and certain other management roles, the range of data collected during the work evaluation phase is very essential. This data therefore differs greatly depending on the purpose and goals of the analysis programme. Job analysis is a key instrument for all organizations in human resources management. The different benefits of work assessment are:

(a) Provides First Hand Job-Related Information : Process of job analysis offers useful data on jobs such as tasks and tasks of a specific work, the risks and risks associated with the job, the qualifications and capacities necessary to do this job and associated information that supports executives.

(b) Helps in Creating Right Job-Employee Fit : Jobs analysis enables the administration to put the correct individual in the correct position.

(c) Helps in Establishing Effective Hiring Practices : The work' assessment enables the manager to establish efficient recruitment practices, as work analysis responds to all possible issues.

(d) Guides Thorough Performance Evaluation : The job analysis enables the manager to assess the work of the employees.

(e) Helps in Analyzing Training & Development Needs : The job analysis enables the manager to help employees to train and develop their skills.

(f) Helps in Deciding Compensation Package : Job analysis enables executives to know the needs of training, who can give training, etc. Job analysis enables executives to decide on compensation packages for particular work needs, as they provide data on tasks and risks.

Process of Job Analysis

Job analysis is as useful is not so easy to make. In fact, it involves a process.

1. Organizational Job Analysis : Job analysis starts with the receipt of relevant employment data. This requires Terry to understand how the work is done, how it is related with other employment and how it helps to achieve the organization's efficiency.

The data is provided by separating background data into different types such as organizational charts, i.e. the association of the specific job with other employment; class requirements, i.e. the overall requirements of the working family; work descriptions, i.e. the basis for building a modified job description and flow chart, i.e. the flow of work involving a specific work.

2. Selecting Representative Jobs for Analysis : It is both expensive and time consuming to analyze all the employment of an organization. For the purpose of thorough evaluation, therefore, only a representative sample of employment is chosen.

3. Collection of Data for Job Analysis : This step collects the work information and the necessary skills of the worker. Either through surveys, observations or interviews the data can be obtained. However, careful consideration should be provided to selecting and using the most accurate technique of information collection in the specified work scenario.

4. Preparing Job Description : Now a job description is being prepared using the work data gathered in the above manners. The work description is a written declaration which outlines the tasks, tasks and tasks to be performed efficiently.

5. Preparing Job Specification : The last stage in job analysis is to prepare work data on the grounds of the data gathered. This is a written declaration specifying personal characteristics, qualifications, abilities, abilities, etc. needed for a task to be performed efficiently. The above-mentioned job analysis method is now shown below.

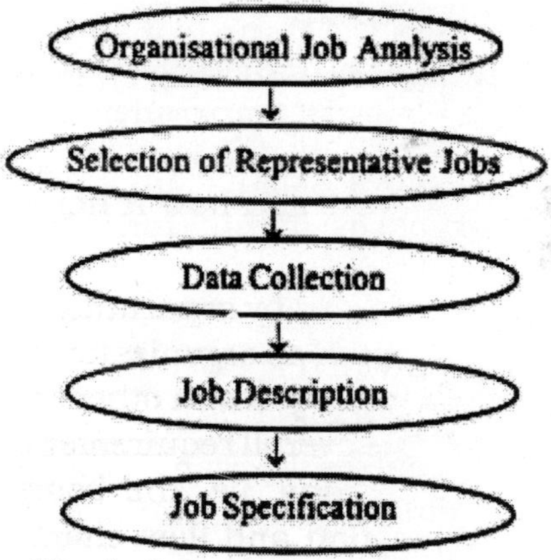

Fig. 1. Process of Job Analysis

***Source*: Primary Data**

Purpose of Job Analysis

As already mentioned, work evaluation consists of gathering and recording job-related information such as expertise and abilities needed for work, tasks and tasks involved, qualifications and experience needed for schooling and the physical and emotional features needed to do a job in the desired way.

The primary purpose of a work assessment method is to use that data to produce the correct fit between a job and an employee, to evaluate an employee's performance, to determine the value of a particular task and to evaluate a person's training and growth requirements.

Let us use an instance to comprehend the notion. The first and foremost thing to determine the value of the job would be to analyze the work of an executive salesman. The next stage is to evaluate whether the individual can deliver what he or she expects. It also enables you to know whether he or she is ideal for this work. Here is not the end of the phase. The reporting structure includes reporting structures, adaptation to a specified setting, management abilities, permits and certifications, capacity to develop and close sales, capacity to manage customer needs, the capacity of the group to manage its own client, its capability to develop and close businesses and its operations.

Job analysis plays a significant role for recruitment and choice, work assessment, work design, decision-making and reimbursement packages, performance assessment, training and growth requires analysis, work value assessment and increased staff as well as corporate productivity.

Job analysis enables determine the kind of individual needed to carry out a specific work. Recruitment and Selection: It highlights the qualifications, level of knowledge and abilities needed for a desired job in a physical, emotional and personal way. The goal is to fit a individual in the correct position.

Performance Analysis: Job analysis is carried out to see whether or not a specific job's goals and objectives are achieved. It enables to decide performance norms, assessment criteria and the output of people. This measures an employee's general performance and evaluates it accordingly.

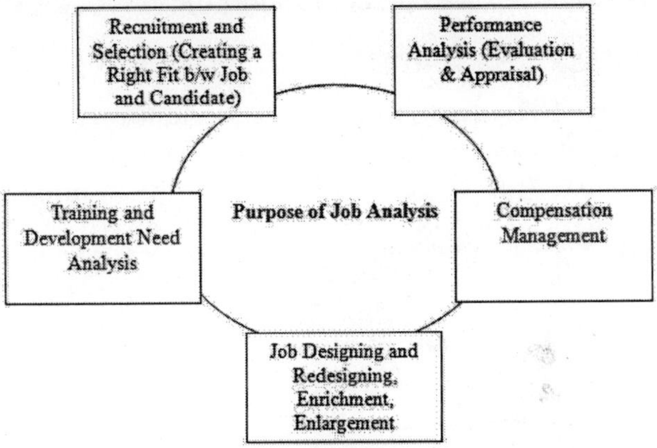

Fig. 2

***Source* : Primary Data**

Job analyzes can be used to evaluate employees ' training and growth requirements. The distinction between the expected and the real production depends on the training level that staff must receive. It also helps to choose the content, instruments and equipment for training and training techniques.

Compensation Management : Job analysis naturally plays a crucial role in determining salary packages and additional advantages and permanent and variable employee incentives. After all, the salary package relies on the job, work title, tasks and tasks engaged in a job. This method leads HR executives to decide the value of an worker for a specific job opening.

Job Designing and Redesigning : The primary objective of the work evaluation is to simplify the human effort and achieve the highest performance. It contributes to design, redesign, enhance, assess and also reduces, and adds additional tasks to a specific task. This is performed to increase employee satisfaction and human performance.

The job analysis is therefore one of HR Manager or department's most significant tasks. This helps to fit the correct talent at the correct moment and location.

3.3. HUMAN RESOURCE DEVELOPMENT

The HR department may demand that the department appoint a main contact individual for all HR issues and build a working relationship to ensure that the required supervisory compliance is ensured. The HR contact with the library should create working relationships with the administrative worker in the library; learn about the structure of the library and what types of problems can occur. Although this strategy obviously deserves, thé staff report to the HR department and not to the library director / dean. The problem with this model is that, instead of the library requirements, the HR expert will still assess the problem based on the task of the HR department.

In light of today's complicated on-campus relations, many academic departments re-evaluate their organizations and realize the benefits of having a resource expert. This inner administrative requirement has been resolved by several academic libraries by establishing an HR role in-house, reporting to library director and interfacing with the HR administrators of different fields. The HR officer of a bookshop works to coordinate every aspect of their specific job problems with its professors, staff and student workers. These individuals may also participate in budgeting and planning as well as in the leadership team, which reports to the director of the library, both on the university and on the administration of this organization.

The job of an HR officer library is different in nature. However, some fundamental features are probable to be included. For academic, professional, classified personnel and hourly employees, the library HR officer is accountable for creating, implementing, coordinating and tracking all human resources and procedures. The human resource officer's age, including jobs, classification, wage management, training and growth for employees and the working relationship. The following could be included in each HR area with specific tasks and responsibilities:

Recruitment : Coordinates professional employees and academic librarians' recruitment, selection and appointment and recruitment of classified workers, teachers and assistants.

Employment/Compensation : In combination with the financial / management bibliotheque, monitor the library's wage expenditures. Monitor annual salaries and market equity hourly wages.

Position Administrator : Oversee position grading and job analysis; coordinate the management process of performance, including evaluations for librarians and employees. Monitor and coordinate the tenure, retention and promotion process of the librarian professors. Ensure the implementation of positive activities, equal opportunities, other federal and state laws and policies on universities and libraries.

Training/Staff Development : Develop and supervise extensive library staff guidance and training programs, including needs evaluation, curriculum design and evaluation. Training may include instructions on safety and security and monitoring of library security activities (e.g. emergencies and processes).

The head of the HR library can also be a member of the leadership team of the manager. This connection guarantees that HR problems are examined in the entire library's strategic framework. This administrative body is also essential to be conscious of the extent to which any decisions it makes impact library staff.

Sometimes there is concern about how a HR library

fits into the organization framework of the campus. Operations at Campus HR usually welcome the development of a functional HR library specialist. With the help of an experienced professional HR, supervising the daily operations of the campus library, the institutional HR department works tightly with one person to guarantee better compliance with the defined protocol on all of the library's functional requirements and freeing the supervision officers of the campus. This connection, on the other hand, enables the library officer in charge of fundamental problems in-house, directly addresses general library problems at the HR campus and represents the library management when discussing associated problems.

Needs of Human Resource Development

In order to attain its aim, staff in an organization need to possess distinct type of abilities such as understanding, knowledge and attitudes in technical and technological sectors, human relations and concepts. Therefore there is a need for an organization to develop human resources:

(a) To survive and to stabilize.

(b) To develop continuously employee skills in an ever-changing work setting well.

(c) To Identify and train employees ' competence gaps in terms of their current and future responsibilities and generate circumstances for employee development to bridge such gaps.

(d) To improve ongoing skill growth for efficient results.

(e) To increase employee motivation for team construction and the environment for cooperation.

(f) To get their job engaged.

(g) To make them constantly want to put their effort into doing stuff.

(h) In the workplace, make them confident.

(i) To encourage initiative and responsiveness.

(j) The team spirit to work together.

(k) To improve quality and productivity

Functions of Human Resource Development in Academic Libraries

The most frequently used Human Resources Development (HRD) mechanisms are:

1. Training and Development : Training and growth are designed to improve or translate library job abilities and methods in distinct libraries.

2. Training : Improving the library professional staff ICT based knowledge, skills and attitudes changing training are following:

Improvement of ICT-based expertise, abilities and attitudes for library professionals:

1. Orientation and refresher courses are offered by Library Professional Staff.
2. Technical skills and training
3. Coaching
4. Training in library management
5. Development Training of Library Supervisor

3. Organization Development : University library employees use the ideas of behavioral science through scheduled measures. In order to accomplish organizational development, both micro and macro modifications are introduced.

4. Career Development : The growth of careers consists of different procedures.

1. *Carriage Planning* : involves work, consulting and skills, to help the professional staff of the library to formulate a realistic career plan.
2. *Career management* : usually; concentrate more on

the measures a company can take to promote the professional growth of its employees.

3. Provision of social services-professional library personnel is medical, educational, recreational, residence, transportation etc.
4. Comments and advice.
5. Work Rotary
6. Team work
7. Development of leadership and
8. Job fortification etc.

Performance Appraisal

The performance assessment of staff, including library and data centers, is an important tool for leadership in every organization. Evaluation of employee performance in almost all organizations is regarded to be one of the prevalent methods. People are hired to achieve the required outcomes and consequently the performance of staff could be considered one of the main determinants of a company's achievement or failure. In organizations, therefore, performance evaluations are essential as they can be used for improving employee performance as a mechanism.

In the past, performance assessment at libraries has been strongly linked to regular library scheduling operations and was mainly used as a written rationale for wage activity. In the past, librarians were immune from assessments of any kind, staff manager of a larger college library in Pennsylvania said; however, with serious budget cuts, she thought that some type of evaluation scheme should be launched. Others who used rating scale assessments said they tried a fresh method. The new technique was often like the one used to assess teaching, especially when the librarians had only lately obtained a professional status. Other library managers, potentially more comfortable with regard to safety in the status of their librarians, have developed methods that specifically measure librarians ' competences or that experiment with management by purpose or mutual targeting.

Training and Development

The term "trainer" is etymologically derived from "trainer," meaning "drag." The most important tool for human resources development (HRD) is training and development. Training & Orientation Programmer is the only and only one way to gain the above mentioned understanding and skills about contemporary technology. Indeed, training and growth starts with particular learning operations, which help the learning process most, and eventually lead to comparatively continuous behavioral change. Training now includes operations, ranging from easy motor skills learning and technical skills acquisition. Training and growth is therefore a significant instrument for the required degree of LHRD to be used successfully in libraries. A workshop, a seminar / conference / convention and a visit to the perfect modern library should also be a helpful instrument for the growth of skills for the library staff, together with training / orientation programs in Refresher courses.

The training and development program should be offered continuously and on a need-based basis to experts, so that they can readily adjust to frequent technological modifications. The skills required in the fresh setting will probably be discovered in a group of skilled talents. The library has another human element, i.e. end consumers. The ultimate goals of the library cannot be a success without the orientation of the end customers. Since everything is designed for end-users, all tasks related to the IT application in their libraries are nothing else than wastes of people, money, time and resources if they fail to use the available resources in their respective libraries Thus, IT applications in libraries can be effectively implemented when libraries tackle clear roles, organizational structures and training.

Motivation

The dominant culture in libraries is that of service, and in public, private or academic libraries this is interpreted in terms of public service. As libraries become more sophisticated in their approach to quality, self-motivation will become a central issue (Rowley, 1996). Libraries must learn to adapt and respond effectively and efficiently to changing demands if they want to survive as viable organizations (Rooks, 1998). It is a commonly held belief that having well-motivated staff is a significant factor in providing an effective library and information service. However, the task of ensuring a high level of staff motivation requires from library managers a range of managerial, sociological, and psychological skills for which they have had little or no training at all. The most important aspect of any organization is its workforce. Motivation arouses, energizes, influences and sustains behavior and performance of employees. Motivating factors include extrinsic factors which pertain to the conditions under which a job is performed and intrinsic motivators which contribute to job satisfaction and subsequently increase productivity. Two levels of motivation were identified in the library: the need factor motivation and the profession related motivation. Need factor motivation is well pronounced in the lower cadre of library staff such as library assistants, clerical staff, and porters who set their priority on economic needs. The profession related motivation occurs among professionally trained librarians whose motivation hinges self fulfillment derived from professional growth and development. Other motivating factor in the library is job design which includes job rotation, job enlargement, and job enrichment. Job design specifies the contents or methods of any job in such a way that various requirements of a job can be effectively satisfied. Adequate motivation of library employees lies with the managers because they generally control work distribution, freedom and autonomy, work challenge Remove, staff development and training, and advancement opportunities. The managers are urged to create enabling environment to ensure improved commitment, satisfaction, and productivity of employees in the library.

Motivating Factors

The problem of motivating employees to increase productivity cannot be resolved alone. Managers are therefore exposed to a broad spectrum of strategies to promote employment engagement in companies. Two groups of motivational variables were recognized as external, or extrinsic, and internal or inherent in Stueart and Moran (1993) and Bakewell (1997) in line with Herzberg's concept of motivators or hygiene factor.

Motivation of library personnel

The library is run by experts who need motivation for ideal efficiency as an organization to meet the data requirements of others across career, vocation and occupation. Dismissed non-motivated data experts would orchestrate catastrophic social effects. The library staffs have a hierarchy from the administration to the porters. To be productive, every employees needs motivation. This concerns the motive of the need factor.

The motivation of need factor consists of human instinct-based requirements. Such needs stem from human and extrinsic psychological needs. Employees are motivated by the need in the reduced framework of the library facilities. This applies to the workforce in non-professional libraries like bookstores, clerics and porters. The main focus of this category of individuals is on financial needs and, as such, work is tied to fringe and concurrent benefits. At this stage, each service is replaced by economic gains and, if the yield is lower than anticipated, motivation is tending to be lost and the output becomes redundant. As a result, these people begin to consider other alternatives, if any. Therefore, cash stays the motivating factor most important as they do not pay much attention to the motive of the profession.

The motivation of the outcomes relates to the professional growth and development. This is especially true of professional booksellers. The reasons for this are indications of development in the professional performance of their tasks. Jobs are controlled by their professional development and growth. This category of staff is motivated by work exercises in the library including promotion, employment expansion, training sponsorship, role definition and headship. Their work depends on self-compliance, linked to professional development and growth.

However, the motivation of library employees is not completely attributed to one single factor; other subliminal factors such as work design are connected with the dominant factor.

Maslow Hierarchy of Needs in Motivation

Maslow thinks that people are driven by unmet requirements. Since each of these requirements, which are organized hierarchically, is met, this no longer acts as a motivator. Only a greater need can motivate workers. Maslow further divided these requirements into greater order requirements and reduced order requirements. The physiological and security demands include lower order requirements. While social / affiliation, self-esteem and self-actualization are more important.

Physiological needs : In practice, appropriate pay, well equipped officers with appropriate ventilation, excellent accommodation equipment (personnel rooms, residential loan) etc. can meet physiological requirements.

Safety Needs : Management can motivate its employees through employment security systems, including excellent pension schemes, insurance schemes, complaint settlement mechanisms, etc.

Social/Belongingness Needs : Those needs can be met by working with teams, associations in the workplace, social interaction, the social welfare package, identification with employer in times of joie and distress.

Esteem Needs : Means Work titles, large departments, difficult jobs, and other possibilities to promote a feeling of achievement can be fulfilled.

Self-actualization : its need can be met by creating possibilities for library management to allow its employees to reach the required height and growth.

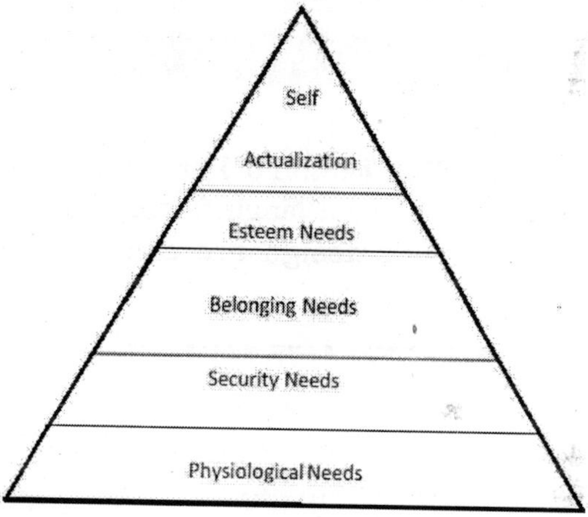

Fig. 3

***Source* : Adapted from Abraham H. Maslow, "A theory of Human Motivation", Psychological Review, Vol. 50, 1943, pp 374-396**

REVIEW QUESTIONS

1. Write a short note on HRM.
2. What is HRM selection?
3. Explain the functions of HRM.
4. Write briefly the recruitment of HRM.
5. Examine the HRM policy and staffing

4

Financial Management and Total Quality Management

LEARNING OBJECTIVES

After studying this unit, you will be able to:

- Understand the sources of library finance
- Know the budgeting procedure and accounts
- Discuss the all types of budgeting like: Line, ZBB, PPBS.
- Know the total quality management (TQM) in the library.
- To understand the experiences of library adopting in TQM methods.

INTRODUCTION

Financial Management means arranging, sorting out, coordinating and controlling the financial exercises, for example, acquisition and usage of assets of the venture.

It means applying general management standards to the financial assets of the undertaking.

Scope/Elements

Investment decisions : incorporates investment in fixed resources (called as capital planning). Investment in current resources is likewise a piece of investment choices called as working capital choices.

Financial decisions : They identify with the raising of account from different assets which will rely on choice on the kind of source, a time of financing, cost of financing and the profits in this way.

Dividend decision : The finance administrator needs to take choice with respect to the net benefit conveyance. Net benefits are commonly partitioned into two:

Dividend for shareholders : Profit and its pace must be chosen.

Retained profits : Measure of held benefits must be settled which will rely on development and enhancement plans of the venture.

Objectives of Financial Management

The financial administration is commonly worried about obtainment, designation and control of budgetary assets of a worry. The goals can be-

- To guarantee customary and satisfactory supply of assets to the worry.
- To guarantee satisfactory comes back to the investors. Which will rely on the earning limit; advertise cost of the offer, and the desires for the investors.
- To guarantee optimum funds utilization. When the assets are obtained, they ought to be used in greatest conceivable manner at any rate cost.
- To guarantee safety on speculation, i.e., assets ought

to be put resources into safe endeavors so satisfactory pace of return can be accomplished.

- To plan a sound capital structure-There ought to be sound and reasonable arrangement of capital with the goal that equalization is kept up among debt and equity capital.

Functions of Financial Management

1. Estimation of capital requirements : A finance manager needs to make estimation concerning capital necessities of the organization. This will rely on anticipated expenses and benefits and future projects and policies of a concern. Estimations must be made in a sufficient way which increments the earning capacity of enterprise.

2. Determination of capital composition : When the estimation has been made, the capital structure must be chosen. This includes short- term and long- term debt equity analysis. This will rely on the extent of value capital an organization is having and extra subsidizes which host to be raised from outside gatherings.

3. Choice of sources of funds : For additional assets to be secured, an organization has numerous options like-

- Issue of debentures and shares.
- Loans to be taken from banks and budgetary establishments
- Public deposits to be attracted like type of bonds.

Decision of factor will rely upon relative demerits and merits of each source and time of financing.

4. Investment of funds : The finance manager needs to choose to distribute assets into gainful endeavors so that there is safety on venture and standard returns is conceivable.

5. Disposal of surplus : The net profits choices must be made by the finance manager. This should be possible in two different ways:

- ***Dividend declaration*** : It incorporates distinguishing the pace of profits and different advantages like reward.
- ***Retained profits*** : The volume must be chosen which will rely on expansion, innovational, enhancement plans of the organization.

6. Management of cash : Finance manager needs to settle on choices concerning money the executives. Money is required for some, reasons like payment of wages and compensations, installment of power and water charges, installment to lenders, meeting ebb and flow liabilities, upkeep of enough stock, buy of crude materials, and so forth.

7. Financial controls : The finance manager has not exclusively to design, secure and use the assets however he additionally needs to exercise control over finances. This should be possible through numerous strategies like financial forecasting, cost and profit control, and ratio analysis, and so forth.

4.1. SOURCE OF FINANCE

This section gives a review of the different sources from where assets can be secured for beginning as likewise for maintaining a business. It also discusses the limitations of various sources and advantages and points out the factors that determine the choice of a suitable source of business finance. It is significant for any individual who needs to begin a business to think about the various sources from where cash can be raised. It is additionally critical to know the relative demerits and merits of various sources so decision of a fitting source can be made.

Meaning, Nature and Significance of Business Finance

Business is worried about the creation and dissemination of merchandise and enterprises for the fulfillment of necessities of society. For carrying out various activities, business requires cash. Finance, in this manner, is known as the existence blood of any business. The prerequisites of assets by business to carry out its various activities are called business finance. A business cannot work except if sufficient assets are made accessible to it. The underlying capital contributed by the business visionary isn't constantly adequate to deal with every budgetary necessity of the business. A specialist, in this way, needs to search for various different sources from where the requirement for assets can be met. A reasonable evaluation of the budgetary needs and the distinguishing proof of different wellsprings of account, in this manner, is a huge part of maintaining a business organization. The requirement for assets emerges from the phase when a business person settles on a choice to begin a business. A few assets are required quickly state for the buy of plant and hardware, furniture and other fixed resources. Similarly, a few assets are required for everyday activities, state to buy crude materials, pay compensations to representatives, and so forth. Likewise when the business grows, it needs funds. The financial related needs of a business can be classified as follows:

(a) Fixed capital requirements : In order to begin business, funds are required to buy fixed resources like land and building, plant and apparatus, and furniture and installations. This is known as fixed capital prerequisites of the venture. The assets required in fixed resources remain put resources into the business for a long period of time. Diverse business units need fluctuating measure of fixed capital relying upon different factors, for example, the nature of business, and so on. A trading concern for instance, may require modest quantity of fixed capital when contrasted with an manufacturing concern. Moreover, the requirement for fixed capital venture would be more noteworthy for an enormous endeavor, when contrasted with that of a small enterprise.

(b) Working capital requirements : The financial

prerequisites of an enterprise do not end with the acquisition of fixed resources. Regardless of how little or enormous a business is, it needs assets for its everyday activities. This is known as working capital of an enterprise, which is utilized for holding current resources, for example, supply of material, charges receivables and for gathering current costs like salaries, compensation, taxes, and rent. The measure of working capital required shifts starting with one business concern then onto the next relying upon different components. A business unit selling products on layaway, or having a moderate deals turnover, for instance, would require all the more working capital when contrasted with a concern selling its merchandise and ventures on money premise or having a speedier turnover. The necessity for fixed working capital increments with the development and extension of business. On occasion extra assets are required for redesigning the innovation utilized with the goal that the expense of generation or activities can be diminished. Similarly, larger funds might be required for building higher inventories for the festive season or to meet momentum obligations or expand the business or to move to another area. It is, therefore, important to evaluate the different sources from where funds can be raised.

Classification of Sources of Funds

If there should arise in an occurrence of restrictive and association concerns, the assets might be raised either from individual sources or borrowings from banks, companions and so forth. If there should arise an occurrence of organization type of association, the various sources of business account which are accessible might be classified as given in Table 8.1 As appeared in the table, the sources of assets can be ordered utilizing distinctive premise viz., based on the period, source of generation and the possession. A concise clarification of these orders and the sources is given as follows:

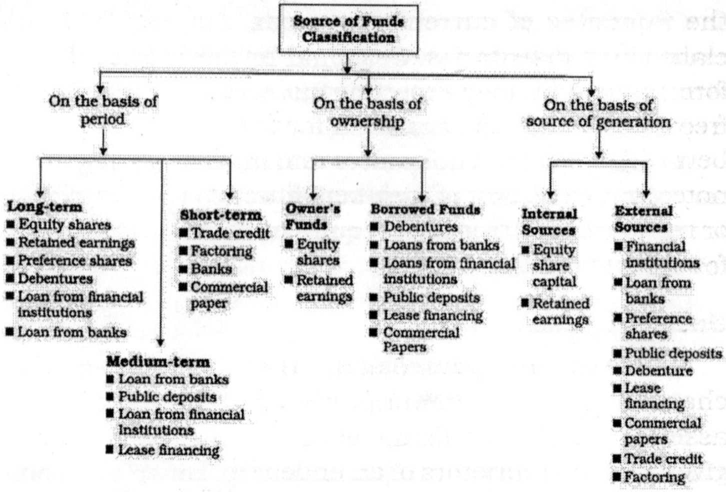

Fig. 1. Classification of Sources of Funds

Period Basis

Based on the period, the various sources of assets can be ordered into three sections. These are long term sources, medium-term sources, and short-term sources.

The long term sources satisfy the financial related prerequisites of an endeavor for a period surpassing 5 years and incorporate sources, for example, offers and debentures, long term borrowings and credits from budgetary organizations. Such financing is commonly required for the procurement of fixed resources, for example, hardware, plant, and so on. Where the assets are required for a time of over one year yet under five years, medium-term sources of fund are utilized. These sources incorporate borrowings from commercial banks, open stores, rent financing and credits from money related foundations.

Short term sources are those which are required for a period not surpassing one year. Exchange credit, advances from commercial banks and commercial papers are a portion of the instances of the sources that give assets to brief term. A short term source is most basic for the financing of current resources, for example, debt claims and inventories. Seasonal businesses that must form inventories fully expecting undercutting prerequisites frequently need term financing for the interval time frame between seasons. Wholesalers and manufacturers with a noteworthy segment of their benefits tied up in inventories or receivables additionally require huge measure of assets for a short period.

Ownership Basis

Based on possession, the sources can be characterized into 'proprietor's assets' and 'acquired assets'. Proprietor's finances means supports that are given by the proprietors of an endeavor, which might be a sole dealer or accomplices or investors of an organization. Aside from capital, it likewise incorporates benefits reinvested in the business. The proprietor's capital remains put resources into the business for a more drawn out term and is not required to be refunded during the existence time of the business. Such capital structures the premise on which proprietors get their privilege of control of the executives. Issue of value shares and held income are the two significant sources from where proprietor's assets can be acquired.

'Acquired assets' then again, allude to the assets raised through credits or borrowings. The sources for raising acquired assets incorporate advances from commercial banks, advances from money related establishments, issue of debentures, public deposits and exchange credit. Such sources give assets to a predefined period, on specific terms and conditions and must be reimbursed after the expiry of that period. A fixed pace of intrigue is paid by the borrowers on such assets. Now and again it puts a great deal of weight on the business as installment of premium is to be made notwithstanding when the profits are low or when misfortune is brought about. For the most part, acquired assets are given on the security of some fixed resources.

Source of Generation Basis

Another premise of ordering the source of assets can be whether the assets are produced from inside the association or from outside sources. Internal sources of assets are those that are produced from within the business. A business, for instance, can produce reserves inside by quickening gathering of receivables, discarding surplus inventories and furrowing back its benefit. The internal sources of assets can satisfy just restricted needs of the business.

External sources of assets incorporate those sources that lie outside an association, for example, investors, lenders, and suppliers. At the point when huge measure of cash is required to be raised, it is for the most part done using external sources. External assets might be expensive when contrasted with those raised through internal sources. At times, business is required to contract its advantages as security while getting assets from external sources. Issue of debentures, getting from commercial banks and financial related establishments and accepting public deposits are a portion of the instances of external sources of assets regularly utilized by business associations.

Sources of Finance

A business can raise assets from different sources. Every one of the source has one of a kind qualities, which must be appropriately seen with the goal that the best accessible wellspring of raising assets can be distinguished. There is definitely not a solitary best source of assets for all associations. Contingent upon the circumstance, reason, cost and related hazard, a decision might be made about the source to be utilized. For instance, if a business needs to raise assets for gathering fixed capital necessities, long term assets might be required which can be brought up in the type of possessed assets or acquired assets. Likewise, if the intention is to meet the everyday prerequisites of business, the short term sources might be tapped. A brief depiction of different sources, alongside their preferences and confinements is given beneath.

Need of Financial Management in University Library

Due to the multidisciplinary nature of studies, document accessibility in multiple fonts, ever rising prices and the insufficient budget, the increasing data demands of customers have made the economic management of the library a difficult task. Financing resources are declining today but specialization in different fields and emergence of fresh and interdisciplinary study areas have increased users ' complexity and enormous pressure for better facilities and resources. The library must meet the requirements for adequate funding because of all these variables. The discussion of the financing of university libraries in developing nations is focused on three major problems. First, the increasing demand for colleges in developing nations and the correspondingly increase level of enrolment. Secondly, the explosion in the number of materials released to promote education and research in universities. Third, the fast advent and growth of digital data enables us to consider radically distinct ways in which library collections are organized than traditionally available, but which in its implementation pose a major economic challenge"*. In the period of the explosion of data, the published literature increased exponentially and the topic became interdisciplinary. Needs have arisen for both Indian and foreign books and newspapers. This has led to a growing amount of books, newspapers, newspapers; work papers etc. These resources have been transferred much more quickly to the university library. "When the digital environment arrived in the mid-1990s and the hybrid library system emerged, the environment of library services and the data services have become more complicated and fresh administrative and economic demands emerge."

Globalization of knowledge and data takes place through the integration of computer and communication techniques. Web and electronic publication introductions influence library collection and services. Technologies used in the past were mainly easy and manual, but today they are complicated. Libraries and data officers must be supported by computer communication professionals and network professionals. If libraries are automated, guaranteed sources of financing should be provided. Automation is costlier than manual processes. INFLIBNET funds college libraries in India to obtain PCs and other associated infrastructures, to hire a data researcher, and thus to set up the library in an INFLIBNET laboratory. The funds provided under the aid program are however not sufficient to completely automate the operations and functions of the university library. UNESCO (1998) states that".

In many developing nations the financial condition means that many college libraries have no means to buy data resources, which have had a adverse and harmful impact on teaching and study capacity. However, academic libraries in India are currently facing many issues as book costs on the global market rise, the increase in periodicals' subscription prices, the increase in conversion rates, but university subscription budgets do not boost as they are. Increasing importance and demand for data, which keeps exerting pressure on libraries, has also gradually led to a change from the need to accumulate and own funds for data to the provision of access. Due to the increasing demand for up-to-date and customer-specific data services such services were needed. There has been excellent economic pressure from existing college libraries to deal with this growth. With scary economic resources you are trying to accomplish above modifications. In the lack of sufficient economic assistance, college libraries are finding it very hard to offer their readers coherent quality services. The growth of libraries and their continuing services involve sound financing. Financial management consists of the process of economic assessment and identification, costing and income allocation for funds and operations which enable parent organizations to attain their goals.

Libraries must face the implications of their financial and economic obligations. "The college library is one of the biggest capital expenses on every campus and needs continuing annual investment in order for it to maintain its value and attain its objectives." The assessment of the library's economic requirements is based on the different library operations. In accordance with the University education program and in the context of an agreed budget the primary purpose of Library is to obtain and make accessible the library collection to the user's satisfaction. This declaration gives us a full description of the University Library organization. Whether for library collection or employees those make these services or administration, which library activity needs to be financed? Library needs funding for the collection of libraries, resources are needed to provide facilities to make the materials accessible or to manage the library. The price of all these variables is the necessary library grant. The scale of requirements and the best source of financing to meet requirements will be identified with proper account. The need to manage university libraries financially at this point has arisen. When data is treated as a product, library finance is relatively simple and economic principles can be implemented more accurately. Appropriate funding is feasible based on a proper and efficient economic management estimate. Any assessment of the library's financial requirements must be based on different library operations. The library's function is to acquire and make accessible to the university learners, researchers and employees all books, periodicals and associated materials and data needed to support university educative programs and within a agreed budget. We need funds to provide materials for our users, funding to provide facilities that make those materials accessible and resources are required for the employees to access, distribute and retain such materials. The price of all these variables is the grant that the library needs.

Principles of Financial Management

For effective financial management, some guiding principles are necessary. An understanding of these principles is useful. These are:

1. Simplicity
2. Effective Control
3. Regularity and Farsightedness
4. Flexibility
5. Economy

Simplicity : Financial management procedures should be easy and simple to use. Efficiency and economy are the result of simplicity.

Effective Control : Financial administration can only function effectively when correctly controlled. The financial control technique should be straightforward and simple. Control is also essential for the cost-effective use and channeling of funds in order to achieve little waste and to make maximum use of restricted economic resources.

Regularity and Farsightedness : The financial management programs should have a typical schedule, so that everyone can know what to do at any given moment. For instance, the heads of segments should be responsible for input in preparing the budget for a library, which in turn would expect their staff's collaboration. The preparation of the budget would take time and a timely submission of the budget would be necessary to allow for budgetary penalties. At a specific moment of the year publishers should also receive subscriptions to the present publications. Keeping to a schedule makes progress thinking and preparing easier. In creating financial arrangements, not only current requirements but future requirements must be held in mind.

Flexibility : Financial leadership should take into account the virtues of elasticity in order to learn how to adapt to conditions. Only in emergencies and crises can it succeed. This does not imply, however, that you should unfairly exploit their flexibility. In the use or divert of resources for a certain product there are rules and procedures for the acquisition of books or any machinery. But it should be under the economic laws and processes. This sort of adjustment generally happens in case unused funds in other products are accessible at the end of the financial year.

Whilst these guidelines are helpful in the operation and management of library finances, the executive authorities lay down statutory financial regulations and processes. There is no choice for libraries other than to respect the economic guidelines. Other associated areas that libraries and data experts must be aware of include cost accounting and economics (especially social economics and manufacturing theory), multiple economic management instruments and methods, economies and costs accounting, such as fund flow assessment, ratio analysis, break-up analysis, operating and monetary averages. The range of implementation in the management and data center of the library is appropriate for financial forecasting, capital budgeting, theory of the economy, production theory, costs, etc.

Economy : In all activities and activities the economy should be impacted, especially in economic matters. All measures to prevent unnecessary spending and wasteful use of poor finances should be taken.

Library Expenditure Planning

You now know how a library obtains funding to run its facilities. The second major element of financial management is expenditure. In the research of financial management library expenses are equally important as consumer spending in a person's daily life. As consumer consumption is the end of all economic activity, library spending is also the end of all the library's finances.

Importance of Library Expenditure

Books and surveys are spent by libraries, as are reading facilities, lists and bibliography services, documentation services and data services, etc. They also spend cash on books and periodicals. The goal behind these is to provide the correct reader with the correct document at the correct moment. The cost of the book is generally to meet readers ' intellectual needs and provide the documents that readers cannot and do not want to buy in their individual capacity. In addition, no one can buy all literature in multiple languages and in multiple types from printers from distinct nations, on distinct topics, in separate topics. The library is the only organization capable of obtaining, processing and making this entire literature accessible. All this implies cash and more cash. That's all.

Nature of Library Expenditure

The nature of library spending has three main features. Library is an organization of expenditure: libraries are not income-reduction agencies, as do many public departments. They are institutions that spend and engage in the construction of nations. The cash the library spends is a long-term investment in human resources. Library is an increasing body: the trinity of library papers, readers and employees is increasing ever. It means that the library's demands will continue to grow every day. All of this involves more expenses. Library expenses are recurrent: not only are libraries expenditure and institutions increasing, but also permanent. During an age of education, library services need to keep up a steady pace to meet the customers' academic demands. In other words, there are recurring library spending.

Principles of Library Expenditure

Maximum overall benefit principle: the library is available at the service of various kinds of readers. As a librarian you must therefore be neutral and make sure that your expenditure policy does not benefit any specific person in specific. You should plan your library expenses so that most readers profit to the greatest extent from the use of the library. Advance plan Principle: Library spending should be scheduled in advance so that appropriate and balance income can be allocated to distinct headings and a correct assessment should be made on various items. In order to acquire the required materials, orders should be placed in advance. Last minute shopping should be avoided by the librarian. Fair allocation principle: Library funding for expenditure for multiple kinds of reading material covering several subject regions should be equitably assigned. Science and technology books, for instance, are more costly than linguistic books. In some topic fields, costly reference books are outdated more quickly. However, their principle can be applied in special libraries, since most documents have to be devoted to the literature and periodicals. Usually, for periodicals, 70 percent of the publishing grant is permitted. All these factors must be taken into account when spending library cash. The Economic Principle: This means that you do not spend any item more than the required amount, and your grant cannot exceed the spending. The additional cost could be better expended for buying fresh alternative titles covered by additional topics, and duplication should be prevented.

Classification of Library Expenditure

Generally, capital and other items that happen almost all year round such as publication books, magazines, stationery and post offices, obligation and contingency, wages, library financing, salaries, etc. against present spending show cash spent on houses, expensive machinery and furnishings. You can, however, classify library expenses by heading, e.g.

(a) salaries and wages,
(b) binding,
(c) stationery,
(d) postage,
(e) contingency,
(f) books and periodicals,
(g) furniture,
(h) building,
(i) equipment, and
(j) publications.

Retained Earnings

An organization for the most part does not disseminate all its income among the investors as profits. A segment of the net profit might be held in the business for use later on. This is known as held income. It is a source of internal financing or self-financing or 'furrowing back of benefits'. The benefit accessible for furrowing in an association relies upon numerous components like net age of the organization, dividend policy, and profits.

Merits : The merits of held income as a source of fund are as per the following:

(i) Retained income are a lasting source of assets accessible to an association;
(ii) It does not include any express expense as intrigue, profit or floatation cost;
(iii) As the assets are produced inside, there is a more noteworthy level of operational opportunity and adaptability;
(iv) It improves the limit of the business to assimilate unforeseen misfortunes;
(v) It might prompt increment in the market cost of the value portions of an organization.

Limitations : Retained profit as a source of assets has the accompanying impediments:

(i) Excessive furrowing back may cause disappointment among the investors as they would get lower profits;

(ii) It is an unsure source of assets as the benefits of business are fluctuating;

(iii) The opportunity cost related with these assets is not perceived by numerous organizations. This may prompt imperfect utilization of the assets.

Trade Credit

Trade credit is the credit reached out by one broker to another for the buy of products and ventures. Trade credit encourages the buy of provisions without prompt installment. Such credit shows up in the records of the purchaser of merchandise as 'sundry leasers' or 'accounts payable'. Trade credit is ordinarily utilized by business associations as a source of short term financing. It is allowed to those clients who have a sensible measure of budgetary standing and goodwill. The volume and time of credit expanded rely upon variables, for example, the notoriety of the obtaining firm, the financial position of the vender, the volume of buys, past record of payments and level of rivalry in the market. Terms of trade credit may differ starting with one industry then onto the next and starting with one individual then onto the next. A firm may likewise offer diverse credit terms to various clients.

Merits : These are the important merits of trade credits are as per the following:

(i) Trade credit is a helpful and constant source of assets;

(ii) Trade credit might be promptly accessible on the off chance that the credit value of the clients is known to the dealer;

(iii) Trade credit needs to advance the sale of an association;

(iv) If an association needs to build its stock level so as to meet expected ascent in the business volume sooner rather than later, it might utilize trade credit to, fund the equivalent;

(v) It does not make any charge on the assets of the firm while giving assets.

Limitations : Trade credit as a source of assets has certain confinements, which are given as pursues:

(i) Availability of simple and adaptable trade credit offices may incite a firm to enjoy overtrading, which may add to the dangers of the firm;

(ii) Only constrained measure of assets can be created through trade credit;

(iii) It is commonly an expensive source of assets when contrasted with most different sources of fund-raising.

Factoring

Factoring is a monetary service under which the 'factor' renders different service which incorporates:

(a) Discounting of bills (with or without plan of action) and accumulation of the customer's obligations. Under this, the receivables by virtue of clearance of merchandise or administrations are offered to the factor at a specific rebate. The factor ends up in charge of all credit control and obligation gathering from the purchaser and gives insurance against any bad debt losses to the firm. There are two techniques for factoring - recourse and non-recourse. Under recourse of action factoring the customer is not ensured against the risk of bad debts. Then again, the factor expect the whole credit chance under non-recourse factoring i.e., full measure of receipt is paid to the customer in case of the debt becoming bad.

(b) Providing data about credit value of imminent customer's and so on., Factors hold a lot of data about the exchanging narratives of the organizations. This can be profitable to the individuals who are utilizing factoring services and can accordingly abstain from working with clients having poor payment record. Factors may likewise offer significant consultancy benefits in the marketing, regions of finance and so forth.

The factor charges expenses for the services rendered. Factoring showed up on the Indian financial scene just in the mid-nineties because of RBI activities. The associations that give such services incorporate SBI Factors and Commercial Services Ltd., Canbank Factors Ltd., Foremost Factors Ltd., State Bank of India, Canara Bank, Punjab National Bank, Allahabad Bank. What's more, numerous non-banking money organizations and different offices give factoring services.

Merits : The benefits of factoring as a source of finance are as per the following:

(i) Obtaining assets through factoring is less expensive than financing through different methods, for example, bank credit;

(ii) With income quickened by factoring, the customer can meet his/her liabilities speedily as and when these emerge;

(iii) Factoring as a source of assets is adaptable and guarantees a positive example of money inflows from credit deals. It gives security to an obligation that a firm may some way or another is not able get;

(iv) It docs not make any charge on the benefits of the firm;

(v) The customer can focus on other practical zones of business as the duty of credit control is carried by the factor.

Limitations : These are the limitations of factoring as sources of finance are as follows:

(i) This source is costly when the solicitations are various and littler in sum;

(ii) The development account given by the factor firm is commonly accessible at a higher intrigue cost than the typical pace of intrigue;

(iii) The factor is a third party to the client who may not feel great while managing it.

Lease Financing

A rent is a legally binding understanding whereby one gathering i.e., the proprietor of a benefit gives the other party the privilege to utilize the advantage as a by product of an occasional payment. At the end of the day it is a leasing of an advantage for some predetermined period.

The proprietor of the advantages is known as the 'lessor' while the gathering that uses the benefits is known as the 'tenant'. The resident pays a fixed occasional sum called rent rental to the lessor for the utilization of the advantage. The terms and conditions controlling the rent courses of action are given in the rent contract. Toward the finish of the rent time frame, the benefit returns to the lessor. Rent account gives significant methods for modernization and expansion to the firm. Such kind of financing is progressively common in the securing of such resources as PCs and electronic gear which become out of date faster due to the quick changing technological developments. While settling on the renting choice, the expense of renting a benefit must be contrasted and the expense of owning the equivalent.

Merits : The significant merits of lease financing are as per the following:

(i) It empowers the renter to procure the asset with a lower speculation;

(ii) Simple documentation makes it simpler to finance resources;

(iii) Lease rentals paid by the resident are deductible for computing taxable profits;

(iv) It gives finance without weakening the proprietorship or control of business;

(v) The lease agreement does not influence the debt raising capacity of an enterprise;

(vi) The risk of obsolescence is borne by the lesser. This enables more prominent adaptability to the tenant to supplant the advantage.

Limitations : The limitations of lease financing are given as follow:

(i) A lease arrangement may force certain confinements on the utilization of assest. For instance, it may not enable the renter to make any change or alteration in the asset;

(ii) The typical business activities might be influenced in the event that the lease is not recharged;

(iii) It might bring about higher payout commitment in the event that the equipment is not discovered valuable and the resident selects untimely end of the lease agreement; and

(iv) The lessee never turns into the proprietor of the assets. It denies him of the leftover estimation of the asset.

Public Deposits

The deposits that are raised by associations legitimately from the public are known as public deposits. Rates of interest offered on public deposits are generally higher than that offered on bank deposits. Any individual who is interested in an association can do as such by topping off a recommended structure. The association consequently issues a deposit receipt as affirmation of the debt. Public deposits can deal a with both medium and short-term financial requirements of a business. The deposits are useful to both the investor just as to the association. While the depositors get higher loan fee than that offered by banks, the cost of deposits to the organization is not exactly the expense of borrowings from banks. Organizations for the most part welcome public deposits for a period upto three years. The acknowledgment of public deposits is managed by the Reserve Bank of India.

Merits : The merits of public deposits are:

(i) The strategy of acquiring deposits is basic and does not contain prohibitive conditions as are by and large there in a loan agreement;

(ii) Cost of public deposits is generally lower than the expense of borrowings from banks and financial related establishments;

(iii) Public deposits do not ordinarily make any charge on the assets of the organization. The assets can be utilized as security for raising loans from different sources;

(iv) As the investors do not have voting rights, the control of the organization is not diluted.

Limitations : The major limitations of public deposits are as follows:

(i) New organizations generally find it difficult to raise assets through public deposits;

(ii) It is an inconsistent source of finance as the public may not react when the organization needs cash;

(iii) Collection of public deposits may demonstrate troublesome, especially when the size of deposits required is huge.

Commercial Paper (CP)

Commercial Paper emerged as a source of short term finance in our nation in the mid-nineties. Commercial paper is an unbound promissory note issued by a firm to raise assets for a short period, changing from 90 days to 364 days. It is issued by one firm to different business firms, banks, pension funds, and insurance agencies. The sum raised by CP is commonly extremely huge. As the debt is absolutely unbound, the organizations having great credit rating can issue the CP. Its guideline goes under the domain of the Reserve Bank of India. The merits and limitations of a Commercial Paper are as per the following:

Merits

(i) A commercial paper is sold on an unbound premise and does not contain any prohibitive conditions;

(ii) As it is an uninhibitedly transferable instrument, it has high liquidity;

(iii) It gives more funds contrasted with different sources. By and large, the expense of CP to the issuing firm is lower than the expense of commercial bank loans;

(iv) A commercial paper gives a nonstop source of funds. This is on the grounds that their development can be custom fitted to suit the prerequisites of the issuing firm. Further, developing commercial paper can be reimbursed by selling new commercial paper;

(v) Companies can park their abundance funds in commercial paper along these lines procuring some good return for the equivalent.

Limitations

(i) Only financially stable and exceptionally evaluated firms can fund-raise through commercial papers. New and decently evaluated firms are not in a situation to raise funds by this strategy;

(ii) The size of fund that can be raised through commercial paper is restricted to the overabundance liquidity accessible with the providers of funds at a specific time;

(iii) Commercial paper is an indifferent strategy for

financing. All things considered if a firm is not in a situation to recover its paper because of financial challenges, broadening the development of a CP is beyond the realm of imagination.

Issue of Shares

The capital acquired by issue of shares is known as share capital. The capital of an organization is isolated into small units called shares. Each share has its ostensible value. For instance, an organization can issue 1,00,000 shares of Rs. 10 each for an all-out estimation of Rs. 10,00,000. The individual holding the share is known as investor. There are two types of shares ordinarily issued by an organization. These are value shares and inclination shares. The cash raised by issue of equity shares is called equity share capital, while the money raised by issue of inclination shares is called inclination share capital.

(a) Equity Shares : Equity shares are the most significant source of raising long term capital by an organization. Equity shares speak to the responsibility for organization and hence the capital raised by issue of such shares is known as proprietorship capital or proprietor's assets. Equity shares capital is an essential to the making of an organization. Equity investors do not get a fixed profit yet are paid based on income by the organization. They are alluded to as 'residual owners' since they get what is left after every single other case on the organization's salary and assets have been settled. They appreciate the reward just as bear the danger of proprietorship. Their obligation, in any case, is constrained to the degree of capital contributed by them in the organization. Further, through their right to vote, these shareholders have a right to participate in the management of the company.

Merits : The important merits of raising funds through issuing equity shares are given as below:

(i) Equity offers are reasonable for speculators who are eager to expect hazard for higher returns;

(ii) Payment of profit to the equity investors is not obligatory. Thusly, there is no burden on the organization in this regard;

(iii) Equity capital fills in as changeless capital all things considered to be reimbursed distinctly at the time of liquidation of an organization. As it stands toward the end in the rundown of claims, it gives a pad to loan bosses, in case of ending up of an organization;

(iv) Equity capital gives credit value to the organization and certainty to prospective loan providers;

(v) Funds can be raised through equity issue without making any charge on the assets of the organization. The assets of an organization are, in this manner, liberated to be sold with the end goal of borrowings, if the need be;

(vi) Democratic control over administration of the organization is guaranteed because of voting rights of equity shareholders.

Limitations : The major limitations of raising funds through issue of equity shares are as follows:

(i) Investors who need relentless income may not lean toward value shares as equity shares get fluctuating returns;

(ii) The expense of equity shares is commonly more when contrasted with the expense of raising funds through different sources;

(iii) Issue of additional equity shares weakens the casting a ballot power, and earnings of existing value investors;

(iv) More conventions and procedural postponements are included while raising assets through issue of value share.

(b) Preference Shares : The capital raised by issue of inclination shares is called inclination share capital. The inclination shareholders appreciate a special position over value shareholders in two different ways:

(i) accepting a fixed rate of profit, out of the net profits of the organization, before any profit is announced for equity shareholders; and

(ii) getting their capital after the cases of the organization's creditors have been settled, at the time of liquidation. In other words, when contrasted with the equity investors, the inclination shareholders have a preferential claim over dividend and repayment of capital. Preference shares resemble debentures as they bear fixed rate of return. Also as the dividend is payable only at the discretion of the directors and only out of profit after tax, to that extent, these resemble equity shares. Thus, preference shares have some characteristics of both equity shares and debentures. Preference shareholders generally do not enjoy any voting rights. A company can issue different types of preference shares.

Merits : The merits of preference shares are given as follows:

(i) Preference shares give sensibly relentless income as fixed pace of return and security of venture;

(ii) Preference shares are valuable for those financial specialists who need fixed pace of return with comparatively low risk;

(iii) It does not influence the control of equity shareholders over the administration as inclination shareholders do not have casting a ballot rights;

(iv) Payment of fixed pace of profit to inclination shares may empower an organization to proclaim higher paces of profit for the equity shareholders in great occasions;

(v) Preference shareholders have a particular right of reimbursement over value shareholders in case of liquidation of an organization;

(vi) Preference capital does not make any kind of charge against the assets of an organization.

Limitations : The major limitations of preference shares as source of business finance are as follows:

(i) Preference shares are not appropriate for those investors who are happy to go for broke and are keen on higher returns;

(ii) Preference capital dilutes the cases of equity shareholders over resources of the organization;

(iii) The pace of profit on inclination offers is commonly higher than the pace of interest on debentures;

(iv) As the profit on these shares is to be paid just when the organization gains benefit, there is no guaranteed return for the speculators. Hence, these offers may not be alluring to the investors;

(v) The profit paid is not deductible from benefits as cost. In this way, there is no assessment sparing as on account of interest on credits.

Debentures

Debentures are a significant instrument for raising long term debt capital. An organization can raise assets through issue of debentures, which bear a fixed pace of interest. The debenture issued by an organization is an affirmation that the organization has acquired a specific measure of cash, which it guarantees to reimburse at a future date. Debenture holders are, thusly, named as leasers of the organization. Debenture holders are paid a fixed expressed measure of interest at determined interims state a half year or one year.

Public issue of debentures necessitates that the issue be evaluated by a credit rating agency like CRISIL (Credit Rating and Information Services of India Ltd.) on viewpoints like reputation of the organization, its gainfulness, debt overhauling limit, credit value and the apparent danger of loaning. An organization can issue various sorts of debenture. Issue of Zero Interest Debentures (ZID) which does not convey any unequivocal pace of interest has likewise turned out to be well popular in recent years. The distinction between the assumed worth of the debenture and its purchase price is the return to the investor.

Merits : The merits of raising funds through debentures are given as follows:

(i) It is favored by investors who need fixed salary at lesser hazard;

(ii) Debentures are fixed charge funds and do not participate in benefits of the organization;

(iii) The issue of debentures is reasonable in the circumstance when the sales and income are moderately steady;

(iv) As debentures do not convey casting a ballot rights, financing through debentures does not weaken control of equity shareholders on the executives;

(v) Financing through debentures is less expensive when contrasted with cost of inclination or equity capital as the interest payment on debentures is tax deductible.

Limitations : A debenture as source of funds has certain limitations. These are given as follows:

(i) As fixed charge instruments, debentures put a perpetual burden on the income of an organization. There is a more serious risk when income of the organization changes;

(ii) If there should arise an occurrence of redeemable debentures, the organization needs to make arrangements for reimbursement on the predetermined date, notwithstanding during times of budgetary trouble;

(iii) Each organization has certain borrowing capacity. With the issue of debentures, the limit of an organization to further borrow funds reduces.

Commercial Banks

Commercial banks possess a crucial position as they give assets to various purposes just as for various timespans. Banks extend loans to firms everything being equal and from numerous points of view, similar to, money credits, overdrafts, term loans, Purchase/discounting of bills, and issue of letter of credit. The pace of interest charged by banks relies upon different factors, for example, the qualities of the firm and the degree of interest costs in the economy. The loan is reimbursed either in single amount or in portions.

Bank credit is definitely not a lasting source of assets. Despite the fact that banks have begun broadening advances for longer periods, for the most part such credits are utilized for medium to short periods. The borrower is required to give some security or make a charge on the assets of the firm before a loan is endorsed by a commercial bank.

Merits : The merits of raising funds from a commercial bank are as follows:

(i) Banks give opportune help to business by giving funds as and when required by it.

(ii) Secrecy of business can be kept up as the data provided to the bank by the borrowers is kept private;

(iii) Formalities, for example, issue of plan and endorsing are not required for raising loans from a bank. This, in this way, is a simpler source of funds;

(iv) Loan from a bank is an adaptable source of finance as the credit amount can be expanded by business needs and can be reimbursed ahead of time when funds are not required.

Limitations : The major limitations of commercial banks as a source of finance are as follows:

(i) Funds are commonly accessible for short periods and its renewal or extension is unsure and troublesome;

(ii) Banks make point by point examination of the organization's issues, monetary structure and so forth., and may likewise request security of advantages and individual sureties. This makes the method of getting reserves marginally troublesome;

(iii) In some cases, troublesome terms and conditions are forced by banks. for the award of advance. For instance, confinements might be forced on the sale of mortgaged goods, hence making typical business working troublesome.

Financial Institutions

The legislature has built up various financial establishments everywhere throughout the nation to give finance to business associations. These organizations are built up by the focal just as state governments. They give both possessed capital and loan capital for long and medium term prerequisites and supplement the customary financial organizations like business banks. As these organizations target advancing the industrial advancement of a nation, these are likewise called 'development banks'. Notwithstanding giving financial help, these establishments additionally direct market reviews and give technical assistance and managerial services to individuals who run the enterprises. This source of financing is viewed as appropriate when enormous assets for longer length are required for reorganization, extension, and modernization of an endeavor.

Merits : The merits of raising funds through financial institutions are as follows:

(i) Financial organizations give long term finance, which are not given by commercial banks;

(ii) Besides giving funds, a considerable lot of these organizations give financial, administrative, technical advice and consultancy to business firms;

(iii) Obtaining loan from financial foundations expands the altruism of the acquiring organization in the capital market. Thus, such an organization can raise reserves effectively from different sources also;

(iv) As reimbursement of loan can be made in simple portions, it does not demonstrate to be quite a burden on the business;

(v) The funds are made accessible notwithstanding during times of misery, when different sources of account are not accessible.

Limitations : The major limitations of raising funds from financial institutions are as given below:

(i) Financial establishments pursue unbending criteria for award of loans. Such a large number of customs make the strategy tedious and costly;

(ii) Certain limitations, for example, confinement on dividend payment are forced on the forces of the obtaining organization by the budgetary establishments;

(iii) Financial foundations may have their chosen people on the Board of Directors of the obtaining organization in this manner confining the forces of the organization.

International Financing

In addition to the sources mentioned on top of, there ar varied avenues for organizations to lift funds internationally. With the gap of Associate in Nursing economy and therefore the operations of the business organizations changing into international, Indian corporations have Associate in access to funds in global capital market. Varied international sources from wherever funds could also be generated include:

(i) Commercial Banks : Commercial banks everywhere the globe extends foreign currency loans for business functions. They are a very important supply of finance non-trade international operations. The categories of loans and services provided by banks vary from country to country. For instance, customary chartered emerged as a serious supply of foreign currency loans to the Indian business.

(ii) International Agencies and Development Banks : A number of international agencies and development banks have emerged over the years to finance international trade and business. These bodies give long and medium term loans and grants to push the event of economically backward areas within the world. These bodies were created by the Governments of developed countries of the planet at national, regional and international levels for funding numerous comes. The a lot of notable among them embody International Finance Corporation (IFC), EXIM Bank and Asian Development Bank.

(iii) International Capital Markets : Modern organizations as well as transnational corporations rely upon sizeable borrowings in rupees furthermore as in foreign currency. Distinguished monetary instruments used for this purpose are:

(a) ***Global Depository Receipts (GDR's)* :** The native currency shares of an organization area unit delivered to the deposit bank. The deposit bank problems deposit receipts against these shares. Such deposit receipts denominated in United States of America bucks area unit referred to as Gold deposit Receipts (GDR). GDR may be an instrument and may be listed freely like every different security. Within the Indian context, a GDR is an instrument issued abroad by an Indian company to boost funds in some foreign currency and is listed and listed on an overseas exchange. A holder of GDR will at any time convert it into the amount of shares it represents. The holders of GDRs do not carry any pick rights however solely dividends and capital appreciation. Several Indian corporations like Infosys, Reliance, Wipro and ICICI have raised cash through issue of GDRs.

(b) ***American Depository Receipts (ADRs)*** **:** The installation receipts issued by a corporation within the USA are referred to as American Depository Receipts. ADRs are bought and oversubscribed in yank markets, like regular stocks. It is like a GDR except that it will be issued solely to Americans and might be listed and listed on a stock market of USA.

(c) ***Indian Depository Receipt (IDRs)*** **:** An Indian facility Receipt could be a financial instrument denominated in Indian Rupees within the kind of a facility Receipt. It is created by associate degree Indian facility to change a distant company to boost funds from the Indian stock exchange. The IDR could be a specific Indian version of the similar world facility receipts. The foreign company supplying IDR deposits shares to associate degree Indian facility (custodian of securities registered with the Securities and Exchange Board of India). In turn, the facility problems receipts to investors in India against these shares. The advantages of the underlying shares (like bonus, dividends, etc.) accrue to the IDR holders in India.

According to SEBI pointers, IDRs area unit issued to Indian residents within the same means as domestic shares area unit issued. The institution company makes a public supply in India, and residents will bid in barely identical format and technique as they bid for Indian shares. 'Standard chartered PLC' was the primary company that issued Indian facility Receipt in Indian stock exchange in June 2010.

(d) ***Foreign Currency Convertible Bonds (FCCBs) :*** Foreign currency convertible bonds are equity connected debt securities that are to be regenerate into equity or deposit receipts once a particular amount. Thus, a holder of FCCB has the choice of either changing them into equity shares at a planned worth or rate, or retentive the bonds. The FCCB's are issued in a very foreign currency and carries a set charge per unit that is not up to the speed of the other similar nonconvertible certificate of indebtedness. FCCB's are listed and listed in foreign stock exchanges. FCCB's are terribly just like the convertible debentures issued in Asian country.

Factors Affecting the Choice of the Source of Funds

Financial wants of a business are of various varieties - future, short term, mounted and unsteady. Therefore, business corporations resort to differing kinds of sources for raising funds. Short borrowings provide the advantage of reduced price thanks to the reduction of idle capital, however long – term borrowings are thought-about a necessity on several grounds. Equally equity capital includes a role to play within the theme for raising funds within the company sector.

As no supply of funds is empty limitations, it's best to use a mixture of sources, rather than relying solely on one supply. Variety of things has an effect on the selection of this mix, creating it an awfully advanced call for the business. The factors that have an effect on the selection of supply of finance are in brief mentioned below:

(i) Cost : There are 2 sorts of value viz., the value of procurance of funds and value of utilizing the funds. Each these prices ought to be taken into consideration whereas deciding concerning the supply of funds which will be employed by a company.

(ii) Financial strength and stability of operations : The financial strength of a business is additionally a key dete minant. Within the alternative of source of funds business ought to be in a very thousand financial position soon be able to repay the principal quantity and interest on the borrowed quantity. Once the earnings of the organization are not stable, mounted charged funds like stock and debentures ought to be rigorously selected as these boost the financial burden of the organization.

(iii) Form of organization and legal status : The form of business concern and standing influences the selection of a supply for raising cash. A partnership firm, for instance, cannot raise cash by issue of equity shares as these are often issued solely by a joint stock company.

(iv) Purpose and time period : Business ought to set up in step with the fundamental quantity that the funds area unit needed. A short-run want as an example are often met through borrowing funds at low rate of interest through trade credit, cash equivalent, etc. For long run finance, sources like issue of shares and debentures area unit additional acceptable. Similarly, the needs that funds area unit needed have to be compelled to be thought-about in order that the supply is matched with the utilization. as an example, a long business growth set up should not be supported by a bank draft which is able to be needed to be repaid within the short term.

(v) Risk profile : Business ought to judge every of the supply of finance in terms of the danger concerned. As an example, there is a least risk in equity because the share capital needs to be repaid solely at the time of closing and dividends need not be paid if no profits are out there. A loan on the opposite hand contains a compensation schedule for each the principal and therefore the interest. The interest is needed to be paid regardless of the firm earning a profit or acquisition a loss.

(vi) Control : A particular supply of fund might have

an effect on the management and power of the homeowners on the management of a firm. Issue of equity shares might mean dilution of the management. for instance, as equity share holders relish pick rights, money establishments might lead of the assets or impose conditions as a part of the loan agreement. Thus, business organization ought to select a supply keeping in mind the extent to that they're willing to share their management over business.

(vii) Effect on credit worthiness : The dependence of business on bound sources could have an effect on its credit goodness within the market. As an example, issue of secured debentures could have an effect on the interest of unsecured creditors of the corporate and should adversely have an effect on their disposition to increase more loans as credit to the corporate.

(viii) Flexibility and ease : Another facet poignant the selection of a supply of finance is that the flexibility and simple getting funds. Restrictive provisions, careful investigation and documentation just in case of borrowings from banks and financial establishments for instance is also the explanation that business organizations might not like it, if other options are readily available.

(ix) Tax benefits : Various sources may additionally be weighed in terms of their tax advantages. As an example, whereas the dividend on preferred shares is not tax deductible, interest paid on debentures and loan is tax deductible and should, therefore, be most well-liked by organizations seeking tax advantage.

4.2. BUDGETING: DEFINITION AND CONCEPT, TYPES OF BUDGETS – LINE, ZBB, PPBS

Budgeting is that the method of future business activities by establishing performance goals and put them into a proper plan. In different words, budgeting is that the method making of constructing financial goals for a corporation and creating a thought to attain those goals.

Corporations usually have interaction in 2 kinds of budgeting:

- Operational budgeting, and
- Capital budgeting

Examples of Operational Budgeting

In a business, the budgeting for operations will include preparing the following projections for the next accounting year:

- Amounts for sales
- Amounts for producing goods
- Amounts for each department's expenses
- Summarizing the above budgets into a master budget or profit plan
- Cash receipts and disbursements for a cash budget
- Projected financial statements also referred to as pro-forma financial statements

Once prepared and approved, the budgeted amounts are used as a guide or road map in controlling the next year's business activities.

Example of Capital Budgeting

Capital budgeting involves future comes that overlap many or several future accounting periods. Capital budgeting sometimes suggests that listing every project in conjunction with its money outlays and expected money inflows for every year. The amounts ought to be discounted to their present values and conjointly hierarchic by priority and gain.

Once ready, the capital budget provides a guide for investment in future fixed assets furthermore as composition for the finance of the projects.

What Does Budgeting Process Mean?

Creating a budget is way over management sitting down and developing with performance numbers that they need to fulfill within the next quarter. A budget is admittedly arranged for the company's future. Managers and board members meet and discuss wherever they need to check the corporate in years to return, what markets they need to take advantage of, and what merchandise they need to form. So as to realize any of those long-run plans, the corporate should have to form opportunities and track the progress on the way. That is specifically what a budget will.

Example : By budgeting for the longer term, management will calculate will increase performance and increase the chance of success. They usually begin the budgeting method by setting future goals and analyzing past performance. Once management encompasses a sensible plan of however the corporate has performed traditionally, they will begin creating estimates and performance goals for future expected performance.

The budget does not stop with simply creating performance goals. Management should judge and compare the particular performance with the expected performance sporadically to examine however well shut the corporate is to achieving its goals. If bound departments are not meeting their goals, management should correct the matter throughout the amount, therefore the company, as a whole, will meet their numbers by the end of the period.

As you will be able to see, the budgeting method is way quite merely making a report at the start of an amount. It is associate degree in progress impact to boost the performance of the corporate by trailing actual results and comparison them to specific goals.

Types of Budgets/Budgeting Methods

Budgetary Methods

Each library must work with a budget, no matter how small. The librarian and his senior employees prepare their budgets in most of the libraries according to government budget norms. The budget shall be examined, wheeled, if required, before being sent to the greater authorities for final approval and sanction by the Executive Committee of the Library. The common practice is to follow major organization techniques and processes. Some small libraries may be exempt from the elaboration of a comprehensive budget as a special service of relatively restricted scope. There are a number of budgeting techniques that include traditional budgets in many of the libraries that have discovered a way into libraries in latest years. In the following sub-sections, these budgetary techniques are discussed.

Probably one of the most prevalent kinds of budgets is that which splits expense items, one line-by-one, into wide categories such as books and publications, wages and allowances, facilities, supplies, capital expenditure, contingencies, etc. for each of these wide categories. This is the traditional approach that prepares the budget, which is also known as historical budgeting, taking into consideration previous spending for each item. For each significant product in the preceding year's budget the budget is ready with a tiny rise of 5 or 10 per cent, assuming that all of the existing programs are as good and essential and hence are called an incremental budget.

The other name for budgeting items is Budgeting type of items. It is comparatively simple to prepare, present and comprehend that the benefit of this budgeting technique. It guarantees to some extent that the funding given is spent for the specified purpose. There are certain weaknesses in this widely practiced technique. This procedure does not include an assessment of the performance of operations and services or suggests future predictions. In other words, the sum to be spent in operations and services is not necessarily reviewed. Secondly, it passes without a forward push in the same way as last year. Thirdly, the budget tends to be solidified and reinforced. In other words, budgetary funds allocated to a specific item cannot be spent for any other purpose; that is to say, economic rules would not allow spending to be shifted from one head to another. For example, equipment-allotted funds, when unspent, cannot be transferred, even though fully justified, to the purchase of several major titles in present publications. It emphasizes instruments instead of the achievements of these instruments. It also tends to cover up requirements and ask for more money than is necessary. Most importantly, the future looks lack and the output is not accountable.

Formula Budgeting

In line with economic standards (which will be discussed in the next chapter), this technique attempts to link certain inputs such as served customers, endorsed educational programs and book inventory ratio to parent body's total resources. The formulas are used for both economic and budgetary estimates. It seems like this is a wide, fast and therefore time-saving technique. But the changes to each library and its clients and facilities do not take account of them.

Program Budgeting

This method propounded originally in Hoover Commission Report (1949) has three steps.

They are:

(i) Statement of goals of the organization (i.e. library)

(ii) Complete consideration of alternatives and

(iii) Logical and efficient choices of the best.

This technique, extended by the line-item technique, attempts to answer the questions: what are the cash spent? And how should funds for each program is implemented? And better suited to the contracting economy. The economic plan is therefore provided as job unit or workload programs and sub-programs. The work units are assumed to be measurable and the costs of the work unit are components of the budget of the program.

This budgeting technique focuses on the work of the library and the funds for programs or facilities which the library intends to provide are allocated. For example, if a library decides to offer a Current Awareness Service, the cost of that service is calculated and the expenses estimated (such as employees, materials, publications, overheads, etc.). The budget is therefore ready on the grounds of program costs and the need to proceed, change or delete a program.

A library may also group its main programs or features corresponding to the organizational structure of a library such as administrative, technical, reader, etc. Each of these services may be organized via the purchase, classification, cataloging, bibliographic and reference services, documentation services, data services, and summary descriptions of these tasks or programs and relative expense figures. Different operations of every department are provided for in this sort of budget. This technique offers heads of different departments the chance to measure their needs and monitor their expenses.

Performance Budgeting

This approach to the budgeting of programs is comparable, but the emphasis moves from programs to results. The costs are based on the results of the operations and operational efficiency is under pressure. This technique involves cautious accumulation over a period of time of quantitative information on all operations. To evaluate performance and set standards, management methods such as cost-benefit assessment are used. For example, to determine workforce and material for the works, the data on the number of books collected, classified and cataloged, actual hours for the complete work, and so on are collected.

It highlights the program's performance and operational efficiency. The complete consideration of alternate ways to achieve the goals and the logical choice of the best is based on efficiency, efficiency and cost-benefit assessment. The program is like program budgeting beginning with the declaration of agency goals. The budget would be provided by unit costs for particular activities multiplied by the expected operations quantity.

The benefit of this technique is the focus on the library's service mission. However, quality of service and operations are hard to quantify. This technique only measures amount and not quality, which is quite hard to assess in terms of cash. In reality, the budget allocations for a library-like service organization have little immediate connection to the satisfaction that library facilities provide to customers. Some of the hurdles in budgetary development by this technique are measuring advantages of libraries in Rupees, complicated interrelationship of expenses of separate transactions and nonlinear cost variations for every unit production (marginal / incremental cost). Every year, it could look too humble and ask officials to check each procedure.

Planning Programming Budgeting System (PPBS)

The USDOD (Department of Defense of the United Nations) (1961) initially suggested this technique of budgeting. Budgeting and system analysis are two main components of PPBS. PPBS includes systems analysis, ORs (operation research) and other cost-effectiveness procedures in order to compare expenses and advantages in a more systematic and thorough manner with alternative policy objectives or programmes. This provides a rational basis for decision-makers to choose from different programmes.

This technique incorporates the highest budgeting and performance budgeting of both programmes. Planning is the focus of this technique. It starts with the definition of objectives and finishes with the development of programs or services. A significant part of PPBS is also the control element of measurement, which is essential to performance budgeting. This technique combines the tasks of planning, programs and services, turns them into concrete projects and ultimately sets out budget demands.

There are major differences in practice and the problems in applying PPBS are due to absence of norms for evaluating program effectiveness / performance.

It also suffers from other implementation problems and some critical gaps like

(i) to concentrate on what is going to be done and not how,

(ii) failure to supply a tool,

(iii) lack of mechanism for assessing the effect of different levels of financing,

(iv) Focuses on fresh or significant rises in continuing programs instead of forcing continuing assessment of current programs, and

(v) The calculation of costs is based on planning and programming choices.

Zero-Based Budgeting (ZBB)

The method Peter Phyrr created in the early 1970's calls for comprehensive organizational knowledge, time and preparation. It has much in common with PPBS and is contrary to historical budgetary requirements and emphasizes the need to justify every year each component of the program. It takes a' zero' budget for every program, until the appropriate authority is convinced that the program is worthy of assistance at a defined stage. The increase in the budget is not permitted. ZBB is a method for managing, planning and budgeting that needs every manager to explain in detail his / her whole budget application (this means zero-base) and transfers each manager's burden of evidence to justify why he / she should spend all of this. This strategy involves identifying and developing all operations as "decision packages" and systematically assessing and ranking these "decision packages" preferably using a computer. It does not take the past into consideration, but emphasizes present operations. Each program and activity is described in great detail and without reference to the previous economic needs is established. In other words, every year an application for financial aid has to be made again. Indeed, no activity could proceed because the preceding year was conducted. In other words, the entire budget is justified from scratch.

Steps involved in preparation of ZBB are:

- Activities / programs shall be divided into the smallest level of entity,
- Objective, activity and alternative techniques of each program examined,
- Program, with their purpose, shall be divided into' decision packages,
- Ranking' deciding packages,
- Cut-off points are the overall budget allocation.

ZBB enhances library planning and budgets and helps build excellent leadership teams. It also helps to increase benefit tracking over the years. But a severe issue of enormous time and effort in conjunction with the issues in the development and classification of "decision packages" stops its implementation in libraries.

Levels of Involvement in Budgeting Process

We want buy-in and acceptance from the whole organization within the budgeting method; however we tend to conjointly desire a well-defined budget and one that is not manipulated by folks. There is continually a trade-off between goal harmoniousness and involvement. The 3 themes printed below got to be taken in thought with every type of budgets.

Imposed budgeting

Imposed budgeting may be a top-down method wherever executives adhere to a goal that they set for the corporate. Managers follow the goals and impose budget targets for activities and prices. It may be effective if a corporation is in an exceedingly turnaround state of affairs wherever they have to satisfy some tough goals, however there can be little or no goal congruousness.

Negotiated budgeting

Negotiated budgeting may be a combination of each top-down and bottom-up budgeting strategies. Executives might define a number of the targets they might like hit; however at a similar time; there is shared responsibility for budget preparation between managers and staff. This exaggerated involvement within the budgeting method by lower-level staff might create it easier to stick to budget targets, because the staffs desire they need a additional personal interest within the success of the budget arrange.

Participative budgeting

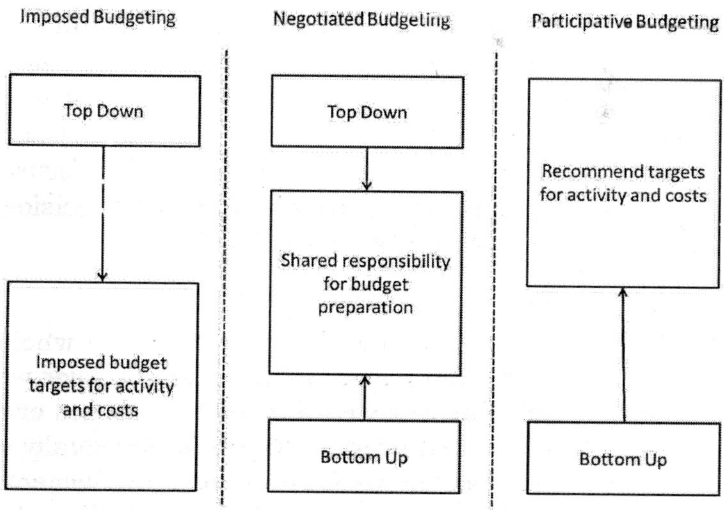

Fig. 2

Participative budgeting may be a roll-up approach wherever staffs work from the lowest up to advocate targets to the executives. The executives might give some input, however they a lot of or less take the recommendations as given by department managers and different staff (within reason, of course). Operations are treated as autonomous subsidiaries and are given a lot of freedom to line up the budget.

4.3. TOTAL QUALITY MANAGEMENT (TQM): ITS CONCEPT, TECHNIQUES AND METHODS

Total Quality Management is an in depth and structured organization management approach that focuses on continuous quality improvement of product and services by mistreatment continuous feedback. Joseph Juran was one among the founders of total quality management similar to William E. Deming.

Total quality management originated within the industrial sector of Japan (1954). Since that point the idea has been developed and may be used for pretty much every kind of organizations like faculties, freeway maintenance, building management and churches. Nowadays, Total Quality Management is additionally used at intervals the e-business sector and it perceives quality management entirely from the purpose of read of the client. The aim of total quality management is doing things right the primary time over and another time. This protects the organization the time that is required to correct poor work and unsuccessful product and repair implementations (such as warrantee repairs).

Total Quality Management is originated severally for a company likewise as for a group of standards that has got to be followed- for example the global organization for Standardization (ISO) within the ISO 9000 series. Total Quality Management uses strategy, information and communication channels to integrate the specified quality principles into the organization's activities and culture

Total Quality Management Principles

Total Quality Management has a number of basic principles which can be converted to the figure below.

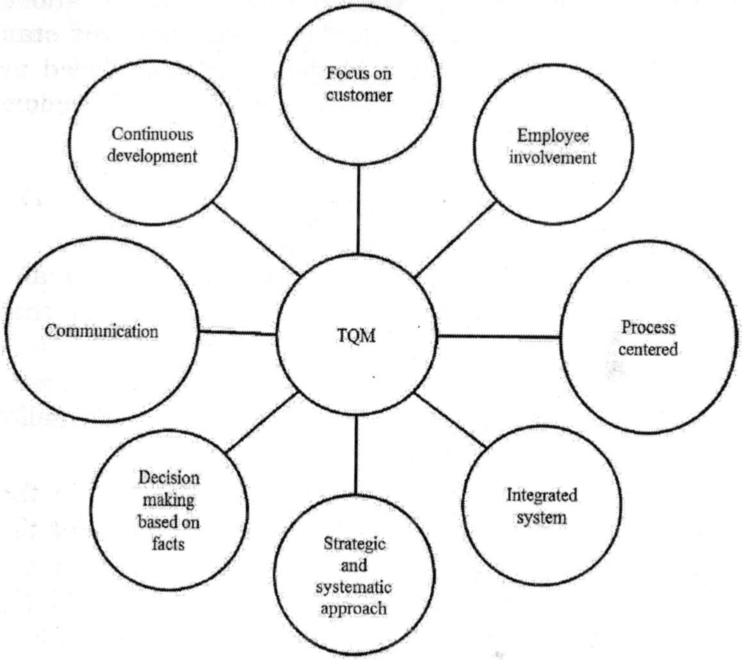

Fig. 3

***Source* : www.toolshero.com**

Focus on customer

When victimization totals quality management it is of crucial importance to recollect that solely customers verify the amount of quality. No matter efforts are created with reference to training employees or improving processes, solely customers verify, for instance through analysis or satisfaction activity, whether or not your efforts have contributed to the continual improvement of product quality and services.

Employee involvement

Employees area unit associate organization's

internal customers. Employee involvement within the development of product or services of a company for the most part determines the standard of those product or services. Make sure that you have got created a culture during which workers feel they are involved the organization and its product and services.

Process centered

Process thinking and method handling are elementary part of total quality management. Processes area unit the tenet and other people support these processes supported basis objectives that area unit joined to the mission, vision and strategy.

Integrated system

Following principle method targeted, it is vital to possess an integrated organization system which will be modeled for instance ISO 9000 or an organization quality system for the understanding and handling of the standard of the product or services of a company.

Strategic and systematic approach

A strategic arranges should embrace the mixing and quality development and therefore the development or services of a corporation.

Decision-making based on facts

Decision-making at intervals the organization should solely be supported facts and not on opinions (emotions and private interests). Knowledge ought to support this decision-making method.

Communication

A communication strategy should be developed in such the way that it is in line with the mission, vision and objectives of the organization. This strategy includes the stakeholders, the amount among the organization, the communications channels, the quantifiability of effectiveness, timeliness, so forth.

Continuous improvement

By exploitation the proper mensuration tools and innovative and artistic thinking, continuous improvement proposals are initiated and enforced so the organization will become the next level of quality.

A supporting Total Quality Management tool that would be used is that the Deming cycle (Plan-Do-Check-Act) or the DMAIC method.

Practical Approach Total Quality Management

- When you implement total quality management, concepts has to be implemented. It is not a system that may be enforced however a line of reasoning that has got to be incorporated into the organization and its culture.
- Practice has tried that there ar variety of basic assumptions that contribute to a booming roll-out of total quality management at intervals a corporation.
- These basic assumptions are:
- Train senior management on total quality management principles and raise their commitment with reference to its roll-out.
- Assess the present culture, client satisfaction and therefore the quality system.
- Senior management determines the required core values and principles and communicates this at intervals the organization.
- Develop a basic total quality management arrange mistreatment the essential beginning principles mentioned higher than.
- Identify and place client desires and therefore the market and confirm the organization's product and services to satisfy those desires.

- Determine the vital processes that may create a considerable contribution to the product and services.
- Create groups that may work on method improvement for instance quality circles.
- Management i,ıtegrates the required changes for improvement in daily processes. Once the implementation of improved processes, standardization takes place.
- Evaluate progress incessantly and regulate the design or alternative problems if necessary.
- Stimulate worker involvement. Awareness and feedback result in an overall improvement of the whole method. Support this for instance by suggests that of a souvenir model, i.e. Management by Objectives, and recognition.

Total Quality Management Techniques

Six sigma, JIT, Pareto analysis, and therefore the 5 Whys technique ar all approaches which will be accustomed improve overall quality.

Total Quality Management (TQM) is an integrative management philosophy for continuous improvement of the standard of an organization's merchandise and processes so as to satisfy or exceed client expectations. There are many TMQ ways accustomed improve business management systems. Considering the practices of TQM as mentioned in six empirical studies, Cua, McKone, and Schroeder (2001) known the 9 most typical TQM practices as:

- Cross-functional product design
- Process management
- Supplier quality management
- Customer involvement
- Information and feedback

- Committed leadership
- Strategic planning
- Cross-functional training
- Employee involvement

The following sections describe some other important and widely used techniques that drew inspiration from TQM in their focus on quality and control.

Six Sigma

Six sigma drew inspiration from the standard improvement methodologies of preceding decades, together with internal control, TQM, and nil Defects. It focuses on rising the standard of method outputs by distinguishing and removing the causes of defects whereas minimizing the variability in producing and business processes Like TQM, the Six Sigma philosophy asserts that achieving sustained quality improvement needs commitment from the whole organization, notably ranking management.

Just-in-Time (JIT)

The Just-in-Time (JIT) methodology could be a production strategy for rising business come back on investment by reducing in-process inventory and associated carrying prices. JIT focuses on continuous improvement to maximize an organization's come back on investment, quality, and potency. The JIT inventory system focuses on having "the right material, at the proper time, at the proper place, and within the actual amount" and defines inventory as a price factor. JIT programs typically embrace attention on Total Quality Control. For instance, once a method or elements quality drawback surfaces on Toyota's production system, the whole production system is slowed or perhaps stopped whereas the matter is restrained. JIT should be organization-wide and consistent.

Pareto Analysis

Pareto analysis could be an applied statistical technique accustomed chooses a restricted range of tasks that manufacture vital overall impact. It uses the Pareto principle: most issues have some key causes. Pareto analysis conjointly concludes that eighty percentage of the result are often generated by specializing in twenty percentage of the key work.

Five Whys

The 5 Whys could be a question-asking technique accustomed explores the cause-and-effect relationships underlying a specific drawback? The first goal of the technique is to work out the foundation explanation for a defect or drawback that points toward a method that isn't operating well or does not exist. The technique was originally developed by Sakichi Toyoda and was utilized by Toyota Motor Corporation because it evolved its manufacturing methodologies. It is currently used inside Kaizen (continuous improvement), lean manufacturing, and Six Sigma.

Importance of Financial Performance Measures

In order to assess the viability of quality projects, results, namely performance measures, must be evaluated. The succcss of fresh projects, such as TQM, with economic performance measures is essential to assess for two reasons: 1) most techniques and investments are justified on the grounds of their effect on economic and accounting measures, rather than operational measures and 2) economic results are the only internal measurement to represent the company's strategies. For these reasons, though the impact of initiatives is not easily valued, the most important measures of the effectiveness of these initiatives are financial performance measures. Financial performance measures show whether the approach, implementation and implementation of the company contribute to the fundamental improvement. Profitability is a matter of typical economic objectives.

TQM and Financial Performance

Many empirical studies examined the links between management practices, quality dimensions and company performance. Adam (1994) investigated the link between alternative approaches to improving quality and operating and monetary efficiency and identified a powerful relation between the strategy and the quality of performance. Terziovski and Samson (1999) looked into the connection between TQM and operating performance, concentrated on the connection between performance and award categories and shown the powerful performance forecasters of leadership, people management and client concentrate. The TQM practice, plant performance, and customer satisfaction have found paradoxical relations between Choï and Eboch (1998). The reasons for variations in elevated and low grade crops were examined by Flynn et al.(1995). The relations between competitive aspects of quality were examined by Curkovic, Vickery and Droge (1999). Sinclair and Zairi (1995) evaluated the outcomes of 22 organizations, which focused their research on the interactions between performance measures, strategic aims and regions of enhancement. They showed a gap between objectives and the measurement of performance that is carried out. In some empirical studies links or correlations between organizational measurements have been discussed. These studies include Norreklit (2000), whose balance record, examined the assumptions and effect chain. In this category there are several studies on how customer satisfaction, value and loyalty relate to economic achievement and on how the connection between staff attitudes and customer satisfaction is related (Bernhardt, Donthu & Kennett, 2000; Brandert, 2000; Edvardsson, Johnson, Gustafsson and Strandvik, 2000).

Similar studies are conducted in relation with financial performance and relations between customer attitudes and market share / financial performance relations between the work environment and customer service (Naumann & Hoisington, 2000). The impact of TQM in the performance of 108 companies that started implementing TQM between 1981 and 1991 were reviewed by Easton and Jarrell (1998). The impact of TQM was evaluated by comparing the performance of each company to a control reference for capturing what performance without TQM would have been. Their findings demonstrated that stock price improvements for companies with more sophisticated TQM technologies were continuously higher (by 16.05 percent). (Advanced TQM systems are based on customer satisfaction principles, staff participation, ongoing enhancement, and long term customer releation).

Quality Assurance

The definition of quality assurance defines quality assurance as' planed deliberate actions or operations instigated and conducted with a view to preserving and improving participating teaching quality.' The definition above does not clarify the distinctive nature of quality assurance although it has been generally understood. According to Frazer (1992), a University which takes quality assurance completely appears as one that is self-critical to a group of learners, teachers, support employees and senior management, all contributing to the quality assurance process and determined to improving it continuously.

Quality Component of Library Services

The Library Committee, which is composed of the Vice-Chancellor as Chairman, the Rector as Vice-Chairman and the Deans of Faculties as representatives and the Librarian as a Convener, is convened to examine progress and issues in library work once every four months. On the basis of the committee suggestions, the library performed surveys with students at the Study Center Libraries on the use of books, reviews and documentation reports by advisors. The study disclosed some significant points, including:

i. Lack of adequate library maintenance facilities in study centers;

ii. Receipt of publications in PG Studies Centers irregularities;

iii. Good use by advisors and students of books / journals and documentation reports.

iv. In view of the problems, Library Committee suggested that the infrastructure for Study Centers ' libraries be improved and that books should be retained.

Reference soft material is subscribed, etc. for the Study Center publications for the Study Centers.

Only then can the university manage its entire quality, which helps it reach its slogan "quality education at the door."

Total Quality Management in Library & Information Sector

Since the development of the topic itself, there has been a practice of Quality Management in Library and Information Sciences but the terminology used for these have varied extensively. Indicators on performance; performance assessment; benchmark assessments using criteria checklists; assessment of information recovery schemes using accuracy and recall rations; cost-benefit and cost-effectiveness studies; user surveys choosing library services views–they all form part of quality assessment research using various assessment and methodology mechanisms.

Numerous auto-validation studies, error rates and trends, which are a control of quality in internet information bases, were carried out in the early 1980s. Customer satisfaction and employees are rarely concentrated. Quality studies have been mainly confined to specialized libraries and scholarly libraries. In the UK, USA or Canada such research is not often recorded in Indian libraries and information systems, although Quality Assurance studies based auf ISO 9000 and other accreditation schemes have been carried out. The quality assurance initiative at LIS is mainly the responsibility of its parent organization. The quality assurance scheme has nevertheless become an essential characteristic of LIS leadership in recent years. In the LIS industry, quality studies are largely isolated, and cover various elements of library administration, service, user research and others. The proof from the few instances of TQM in the LIS industry shows that TQM is an extremely appropriate data leadership concept.

TQM in Distance Education

Although standard and open university libraries share the same fundamental library facilities and features, it requires unique facilities in distance learning libraries owing to the very nature of the distance to students. Limited access to books and publications at the Study Center Libraries are given to distance learners. It is hard to lend books to distance students in practice, as students are dispersed in different locations. The library has therefore to take measures to provide present awareness facilities such as abstract indexes, bibliographic services in order to inform students about new data. In addition to the extra library budget, the selection, acquisition and handling of the books and their transmission to multiple study center libraries also require a adequate number of employment. Assessing these multiple tasks and providing students with feedback is essential for ongoing improvements in the quality of library and data services. Consultants, staff at study centers. In this research the vital criteria are attempted.

Resources

The management must carefully plan for:

1. Financial Resources - For
   i. Central Library
   ii. Study Center Libraries; and
   iii. Regional Library
2. Document and Information Resources
   i. Accessibility
   ii. Preservation
   iii. Availability
3. Technology
   i. Costs and benefits
4. Building
5. Infrastructure
6. Furniture and fittings

Processes

1. Select the facilities required to meet the changing
   i. Needs of the customer
2. Assess services in
   i. Assess services Precision of timeliness of data
   ii. Importance to the goal
3. Service providing cost.

TQM in Libraries

Libraries are the last to embrace TQM methods among the services sectors like airlines, banks, insurance companies and health suppliers. Librarians have long regarded themselves as maintainers of knowledge instead of active agents in the transmission of data. Although libraries' principal aim is to meet the customers, the professional librarians often overlook this. However, today's libraries have to provide high-quality services to their customers to justify their existence. Libraries are now also beginning to adopt TQM methods in agreement with other types of services.

User Satisfaction

While user satisfaction cannot always be equaled with system's achievement or failure, it is often an significant source to highlight the system's and its services ' loopholes. Feedback from learners and professors is crucial if data services are to continue to improve their quality. The LIS services evaluation will assist LIS experts in improving the quality of data services and implementing these services.

Suggestion

Following proposals for the application of quality in distance education libraries are produced based on the above discussions and observations.

1. The TQM University Quality Assurance project should include Library and Information System Quality Assurance.
2. Standards / norms for quality assessment of data services with a special reference to distance educational libraries must be developed.
3. Methods and mechanisms to improve quality information services must be developed.
4. More funding will be assigned for project-based assessment of the quality of data services.
5. Training of employees in quality data services.

TQM in Library

Libraries are the oldest existing social and cultural institutions, with data collected on some sort of medium and retrieved if required. The fundamental aim is to build an organizational structure that collects and makes data wanted effectively available to customers in neede time. Creating and maintaining such a structure and managing large quantities of data that are stored in various formats-printed images, video and sound-needs the most contemporary leadership methods. TQM is a philosophy of leadership that aims at integrating all organizations to fulfill their demands and goals. TQM's application in the library is a helpful way to assess and improve the quality of services in the library. The growing financial difficulties, issues related to the introduction of new information technology, employee issues and increased competitiveness on the information service sector have therefore encouraged fresh approaches to library and Information Management Systems.

The Quality Assurance initiative in the library science industry has been supplied mainly by core or parent organizations. The quality assurance scheme has nevertheless become an important characteristic of the Library and Information Services in recent years.

- Promote fresh services or modifications.
- Developing training materials for users and employees
- Target services or particular organizations.
- Provide delivery of electronic papers.

By using TQM techniques in libraries / information centers, librarians can not only meet the needs and specifications of the user continuously, but also often enhance service quality.

- Improved service quality and customer satisfaction can assist us with TQM in library and information centers.
- Development of an inventory of all library files.
- facilitating searches through a number of

instruments that allow universal publications to be accessible.

- Better resources for the library.
- Increased productivity through effective use of men, machines and equipment.
- Improving the ability and efficiency of end customers to communicate with data systems and services in a profitable way.
- Better management of costs.
- User complaints reduction.
- Removal of bottlenecks and job environment free of stress, which will lead to healthy human relationships and improve user trust.
- Updating and improving workers capacity.

Benefits of Total Quality Management

- Comprehensive quality management guarantees that everything done with a company is as efficient and effective as possible.
- It offers management of market and industry through procedures and systems that encourage improvment in performance which prevent mistakes and stop duplication.
- It guarantees that the organization is compatible with each element of the organization's external and internal requirements.
- Better documentation, better consciousness, beneficial cultural changes and the pride of employees.
- Motivated personnel.
- Better care and satisfaction of customer / user.
- TQM library application improves the library picture.

Barriers to Adoption of TQM in Library and Information Sector

There have been several obstacles to the application of TQM in all kinds of organizations, including the following libraries.

- Inadequate TQM knowledge and misunderstanding of measurement techniques for measuring TQM execution efficiency.
- TQM needs to invest a long-term amount of time over several years while analyzing procedures and changing organizational culture. In these days of increased economic and other stresses, this can trigger opposition and other problems.
- Lack of management engagement and comprehension of quality leadership.
- Lack of knowledge about the advantages of the organization's TQM application.
- Failure to clarify the guidelines, implement plan and techniques of execution.
- Failure to understand the beneficial outcomes of ongoing enhancement.
- User significance is ignored.

Improvement of Library with the Application of TQM

TQM is to define methods for service enhancement of scholarly systems and facilities in libraries. Implementing TQM in library and data services calls for changes in the mental frame of staff and managers of the library; for the segmentation of customers according to their requirements; for a service approach within library limitations to the user section; and without that, assistance from the library's top managers should be enhanced. Implementing TQM therefore needs a change in employees ' approach to their employment. Every worker must do its utmost to achieve the departmental goals that are guided by the library's goals. Everyone must work hard to satisfy and exceed the literature and data requirements of the user. A successful TQM operation requires that the academic library should determine the clients for which a research library is intended to serve, assess their requirements, and choose its services, while maintaining financial resources, employees, records and databases for each user's section.

For effective application of TQM, teamwork is essential. The steady assistance of top management relies on each step in the process. Their function determines the extent to which this can go. A powerful leadership is needed once a decision has been made to apply TQM. TQM offers a template and benchmark for fresh approaches in libraries facing major changes today. The question is whether it is possible to apply the principles without reserve, but methods with appropriate adjustments to the library setting are sensible.

The significance of TQM is product or service client satisfaction. The academic libraries are mainly concerned with supporting their parent organization's teaching, research and other academic programs. A university bookshop is a component of a service organization that provides clients personally. The TQM is currently not a leadership method, but has also found several organizations and disciplines to be very important.

Sirkin, suggests some ways a library might use the principles of TQM to enhance library and information services.

- Service brochures and data kits
- Conduct a library and data services user survey.

Changing operating hours

- Facilitate the return of the material.
- Flexibility in the assignment of employees
- Cooperation with local governments.
- Ask the suppliers to demonstrate their goods

- Give fresh employees guidance.
- Creating consultative groups for the interdepartmental library.
- Enhance the library's physical design.
- Follow-up complaints
- Open satellites office.

REVIEW QUESTIONS

1. Define library finance.
2. Define library budget.
3. Discuss in detail the sources of library finance.
4. Examine on the Budgeting procedure and its accounts.
5. Discuss in detail of TQM and its methods & Technique.

5

Latest Trends in Library Management

LEARNING OBJECTIVES

After studying this unit, you will be able to:

- Understand the concepts, impact, strategies and development of libraries in India.
- Know about Stress Management.
- Know about Time Management.
- Understand the importance of time management.
- Know about Project Management in libraries.

INTRODUCTION

New technologies have continually been of interest for libraries, each for the potential of increasing the standard of service and for raising the potency of operations. In the current situation, once libraries of every kind (public, academic, special, research) are facing economic hardships, the overwhelming reason for considering new technologies is that the potential for value saving in the operations and the management of material flows. Radio frequency identification (RFID) is the technology that is slated to replace Barcodes in library applications. It is a sort of identification that is contactless and will not need line of sight. The technology although new to libraries, has been in use in alternative sectors i.e. in retail and deposit applications since Nineteen Eighties. Libraries began victimization RFID systems to replace the electro-magnetic and Barcode systems in late Nineties. About one hundred thirty libraries in North America are victimization RFID systems, however tons of additional are considering it. As of mid-2007, a calculable 600 libraries with as several as 850 facilities were victimization RFID systems. It guarantees to contour operations by sanctionative quicker self-checkout and self-returns, rising shelf management and inventory management, and providing higher thieving protection. The RFID resolution may be a revolutionary application of automatic identification and information capture.

In some instances through the re-designing and refurbishment of current equipment and in rare instances, through the chance to create a completely new building, academic librarians design new rooms in their libraries. What are the programmatic instructions for architecture and libraries that guide this project and other initiatives in scholarly libraries today? In what amount of room should prints and services be given, and in what way digital services, common data, and other fresh requests on library space should be dedicated?? The responses can be find by exploring emerging "content management" and "teaching space design" library methods which must be connected to the esthetics and function of efficient architecture. Increasing use of Content Management Systems (CMSs) for website management is being made by academic and their parent organizations. To see if internet executives in academic libraries from schools had CMSs adopted, what instruments they were using, and whether they were satisfied with the management scheme for their websites. Other problems have been raised and this organizational level has been the institutional control of the website management of libraries.

Definition

A content management scheme (CMS) is a website content management scheme. Typically the content management application (CMA) and the content service application (CDA) comprise two components: the content management application (CMA). CMA element enables the content manager or author, who is unaware of Hypertext Markup Language (HTML), without requiring the expertise of a webmaster to manage creation, modification and removal of content on a web site. In order to update the Website the CDA element uses and compiles this data. The characteristics of a CMS scheme are different, but most include Web publishing, format administration, review control, indexation, search and recovery. List of Content Management Systems This is a list of noteworthy content management systems for organizing and facilitating the development of cooperative content. Many are constructed on distinct frameworks for content management.

The Technology drives the bus

Appropriate technology should be injected into library areas. Technologies should inform each room in an academic library. The library spaces need to be planned with suitable technological conveniences, from offering more energy outlasts for laptop users to installing complicated 3D simulators. These could include:

- Printing access and wireless Internet.
- Public computers with fundamental software and Internet links that are readily available.
- Distance learning classrooms that offer video and electronic flipcharts for graphical and electronic data sharing.

- Exercise rooms fitted with meeting tables and projection devices.
- Advanced video, graphics, and science-based computing centers.
- Lockers for charging private equipment like cell phones and laptops with integrated outlets.
- 3D visualization rooms such as the false room and CAVE, which enable learners to communicate in virtual settings.

New Progress in academic Library

The modifications to the library scheme focus on the college and university libraries. Academic libraries must provide data and study abilities to groups of consumers. Apart from the difficulties facing the structure of all libraries, academic libraries must also face a quickly evolving climate for education and publication, which questions the importance and costs of academic education. Increased demand for responsibility implies academic libraries need to demonstrate the University system's importance and value. Various organizations have tried to evaluate the effect on student achievement of academic libraries but have often had difficulties with the private sector of employers. The increasing expenses of access to scholarly publications and the rapid expansion of data resources indicate that academic libraries can no longer retain a traditional model of lending and accessions. In addition to the collecting of a big amount of books and newspapers, many university libraries have reworked their physical infrastructure to attract the learners, adding PCs, cups, classrooms and outlets to academic libraries exploring a fresh model of services, known as "digital commons" and/or "scholar commons," which specializes in access, quality of data and literacy.

Academic library collection growth is driven by patron demand and will include new resource types:

Budget cuts, user preferences for access to digital products, restricted physical space and the failure to finance extensive collections resulted in a move from' on time' to' on time ' philosophy for many scholarly books. This shift was facilitated by tailored patron-driven acquisition programs, enhanced print on demand monograph alternatives, a customer desire for emerging kinds of resources and resource sharing technologies such as Rapid ILL, which provide 24-hour turnaround time for product applications. The impact that this shift has on the capacity of academic libraries to satisfy their customers' data requirements are yet to be determined. Libraries also acknowledge the need for digital datasets to be collected, conserved and available.

Explosive growth of mobile devices and applications will drive new services

The requirements and expectations of users will be driven by Smart phones, eBook readers, iPads and other handheld devices. In the ECAR 2009 research of graduation learners and data technology, this proportion is probable for the general population to grow rapidly 51% of participants owning an Internet-capable handheld device, as suppliers provide portable electronic resource interfaces, mobile apps are increasing in OPACs and more libraries provide text message facilities and mobile interfaces for themselves.

Increased collaboration will expand the role of the library

In the organization and beyond collaborative attempts, cooperation with the professors will continue to diversify to include library resources into your curriculum and to pursue guidance in information-literacy and as an integrated librarian. Work with academics to access their information sets, project notes, documents, etc. in Virtual Research Environments and Digital Repositories, working together with data technology professionals in the development of internet tutorials, user-friendly interfaces to local digital collections. Working together with student support services to provide learners with rooted facilities.

Technology will continue to change services and required skills

The most significant technological changes influencing scholarly libraries include cloud computing, enlarged and virtual reality, discovery instruments, open content, open source software and the latest social networking instruments. These advances impact almost all library activities as they do with mobile apps. OCLC's new collaborative Web-scale library management services and discovery instruments are two interesting developments that offer various resources a single interface, with a centralized consolidated index promising quicker and better outcomes than federated searches.

Content Creation

Web for Information Work: For a multitude of distributed data resources, the Internet functions as a worldwide highway, from the distinct ways to host and access these resources. As the dominant internet player, World Wide Web (WWW) can be regarded as the hypertext source web of web servers readily recognizable through recognized URLs and accessed through chips / free browsers like the Netscape Explorer (universal resource locator).

The Basic Step in hosting a functional web site is.

Web Server configuration : A PC or a good Internet linked server with normal software.

Content recognition : what is to be distributed through the web to the outside world.

Build web pages : How to use a web friendly means, by an HTML editor, to represent content.

Web pages upload : server hosting of websites.

Open source software of Library

1. Green Stone
2. KOHA
3. D-Space
4. LINUX
5. E Print Archives
6. My SQL
7. SOUL
8. Jawa
    1. Jawa packages /bundle
    2. Microsoft ASP.NET
    3. Perl
    4. PHP
    5. Python
    6. Ruby on Rails
    7. Cold fusion Markup Language (CFML)
    8. Software as services (SAAS)
    9. Proprietary Software

This chapter lists proprietary software that is installed and administered on the own server of a user. This chapter contains proprietary software freeware.

New Trends

Based on the projects of the businesses mentioned below, some conclusions can be drawn about the trends for e-contents that will dominate 2014:

1. Self-publication is still on the rise.
2. Children are increasingly reading e-books.
3. Lines blur with the expansion of supplier positions.
4. There is greater interest in publishing and owning contents in public libraries.

5. Multi-media component integration is the next boundary.
6. Coming around are trade publishers.
7. The importance of e-learning instruments is recognized by academic publishers.
8. Content still needs to be free (to the user).

Integration of multi-media components is the next frontier

It's a brainless thing. Many studies, surveys and articles have shown that digital reading is interactive at its best. This describes why several sellers develop interactive digitally-born content that invites learners and scientists to learn a fresh way: watching and listening while reading. All digital audio books are also becoming increasingly interested. On this front Baker & Taylor has taken excellent steps, allowing library managers to buy and download digital audio books directly to their mobile phones in Apple and Android.

Content still wants to be free (to the user)

Well, it's obviously. Because we always get frcer access to it, both anticipated sources, such as Open Access Un Glue projects. The Digital Public Library of America (DPLA) and fewer probable sources, such as profits-oriented academic publishers, were uncovered and freshly introduced. Last month, Google's long-term suit (which accused Google of copying millions of books without permission) was rejected as a greatest confirming the value of free access in the 21st century. "I think," the United States said. Judge Denny Chin, Circuit, "Google Books offers important advantages to the public.

Contents Creation in Indian Scenario

- Digital Library of In a (DLI)
- Traditional Knowledge Digital Library
- Indira Gandhi National center for Arts

- Vidyanidhi : Digital Library and E-Scholarship Portal
- National Library of India
- Parliament of India
- TIFR Digital Library
- Information and Library Network
- Digital South Asia Library
- DEL Net ? EAR NET

Implementation of Open Source Software (R&D)

Open Source software is computer programming which provides the source code to the public for free use of changes in original design, i.e. open. There is no worldwide open source software.

- CCF To MARC21 Conversion Utility
- Excel to MARCXML Conversion Utility
- Web 2.0 and Library 2.0 @ INFLIBNET
- Blogs
- Wiki Application Programming Interface (API)
- Subject Gateway management System (SGMS)
- Dewey Decimal Classification (DDC) search
- Search Cloud Computing
- Info Portal: A Subject Gateway (INFOPORTAL -2014
- Shodhganga : Shodhganga (2014)
- Pathshalə (MHRD-2014)
- UGC Info net Digital library Consortium
- Institutional Repositories (evolving).

Emerging trends

Key issues and trends can be observed as challenges for libraries and leaders as well, these challenges may include:

- It is not simple for libraries and librarians to open access content, to select and to access library customers. This open access trend requires competence in content browsing, rulers must update their abilities and abilities, at the same moment as discovery and resource significance for library customers are questioned, and the academic library requires policy and procedural enhancements to the maintenance and offer of open access materials, including maintaining an current institutional repair.

- Modifying wise communication requires a range of fresh abilities to lead the library, and new forms of communication are becoming highly essential for the libraries. Employers are increasingly concerned about providing effective leadership in academic libraries, because organizations need to create fresh approaches to promote traditional technique of scholarly interaction more quickly than ever to tackle emerging challenges (Dewey 2005). Increasing requirements on the digital environment need maintenance for digital material at all levels in academic libraries.
- The need for a redesign in university libraries as a demand for a remodeling scheme of schooling and scholarly libraries is changing in a fluctuating setting (Moropa 2010). The academic libraries are confronted with the challenges of teaching communities because they need a range of areas, facilities and furnishings, combined study room, conference rooms, flexibility in the use of space, relaxation and being an entirely one-stop shop in university life (Chan and Spodick, 2014).
- Declining use of internet library catalogs is causing evolving competitive patterns among other data suppliers such as Amazon and Google; the challenge for the scholarly library was rising (Law, 2009).
- Shrinking library budgets are a major challenge for libraries' future. Financial support for libraries and

leaders is also an continuing problem. At the same moment, librarians have a restricted budget as well as selection and collection development issues (Riggs, 2001; Neufeld, 2014).

- Turock (2003) defined academic organizations as having a broader population each year, and bookstores require more varied leadership to operate in the 21st century. Consumers seek data from huge open access contents because they take online lessons both from far away and on campus; for that purpose, they require library resources online to be used remotely, 24/7. This implies that libraries must satisfy and promote their data requirements in a digital environment without limitations on access to data (Weiner et al., 2009; Moropa, 2010).

In any case, there are a number of evolving trends and difficulties for library managers, and not only for the managers of libraries, but also for libraries, including data storage, the development of robust collection, licensing and access, reduced budgets, data collection and use, data supply, institutions on all levels, in academic libraries. Academic libraries require leadership in the development of fresh strategies, policies and methods to address the difficulties and problems of the education system's reorganization. In the last three decades there have been numerous developments in libraries and these changes are the results of emerging technology trends, and their results are how researchers, students and faculty see the academic libraries, and a clear vision of technology, resources, and services is needed in the near future. The College and Research Library Association (ACRL) reports on these types of modifications have been discussed in recent years (CRRC 2014).

Libraries evolve continuously to satisfy the requirements of their various groups. Far from being an easy repository of books and media, libraries today serve for everything from data analysis to 3D printing, as well as starting coding classes.

In 2018 and beyond, the modern library needs to take into account and react to the evolving faces of its customers. Each population is distinct, but the contemporary library is able to react to latest trends and provide creative and useful data and resources for its customers in numerous respects.

Technology

Image ALT Text : A robotic hand prototype.

According to the Top Technology Trends Resource of the American Library Association, libraries spend $1.8 billion globally on technology. Often these services give users access to fresh products in first hand. A common way for libraries to make fresh techniques more accessible is through manufacturer's rooms. Maker spaces include tech-like content creation laboratories for virtual reality, 3D printer, instruments for product manufacturing, PCB friction machine, laser cutters, etc.

Maker spaces can serve many valuable purposes including:

- Facilitating the development of prototypes for businesses and inventors.
- Science and Technology Professional Education.
- Promoting the resolution of creative issues.
- Providing possibilities for experiential learning.

Professionals of library science should endeavor to create spaces for manufacturers and other technology laboratories that address the various demographic requirements. Maker rooms can consist of complete on-site laboratories, portable carts or even backpacks full of loanable instruments.

Gamification

Gamification is an evolving trend in which learning is framed in a game's easy to access format. From elementary school education to professional training games are increasingly used. Mastery in gambling helps encourage numerous abilities, including in mathematics.

Players can look for guides and manuals in the library to improve their gameplay. In an article published by Wired, Brecht Vanden broucke examined how video games encourage the kids to read, and pointed at the Flesch-Kincaid Reading Easy Guide, the Ultimate Player Guide, between grades 8 and 11, but many bookings like this are damaged by kids of primary age who have their interest in games like Mine Handwerk. By providing the correct literature, libraries can encourage players to learn about the games they're interested in.

Libraries can also serve as a chance for players to socialize through gaming. The Darien Library operates its own craft server in Connecticut. A build-off of a mine was hosted by the Hudson Library in Ohio. Promoting co-play sin pairs, organizations or schools can assist libraries encourage players to jointly investigate different aspects of the game by asking questions, exchanging ideas and jointly processing fresh findings.

Virtual Reality

The technology of virtual reality (VR) gives the user the headset, which takes them up, down and round to immersive locations by merely shifting the heads. Libraries were critical points of access to fresh technologies for a long time. When fresh inventions were still made with computers and the Internet, the local library is often the simplest location to get online for customers.

Today, libraries can give their first interactions with virtual reality to their customers. Oculus has initiated an initiative in California that provides a total of 100 Oculus Rift headsets and pcs in 90 libraries. This technology may not yet be available for the average customer with a cost tag of approximately $1,500 for a headset and VR-ready PC. Libraries with this kind of technology can however assist fresh consumers to acclimate devices that already fall in cost, even if they experience the collection of museums or exotic destinations on a remote basis via VR.

Coding

Library literacy lessons on subjects such as word processing, spreadsheets and internet use are relatively prevalent for libraries. Today, there is excellent demand from several installations for sophisticated courses, especially those exploring coding. These courses are popular with clients of every age.

"Today, the children grow with an iPad in their hands, tells Alex Giannini, director of the digital experience in the Westport Public Library in Connecticut. They do not have to know the digital language; they were born with it. "He notes further that providing coding lessons at a younger era helps these knowledgeable young people understand deeper technological ideas.

Coding courses for libraries across the nation have been effective from the California Berkeley Public Library to the Orlando County Library System. These offers bring in new employers and give regulars, who want to know something new, precious resources.

Social Media

It is essential for libraries to establish, maintain and expand a social media presence. "Our consumers live in a digital globe. This is an significant connecting room." Gregg Dodd, Marketing Manager, Metropolis Library, obviously describes the importance of a digital strategy.

Connections to social media create library events, events and offers easy to share. Digital content like historical pictures are also ready to be shared socially. Bibliothèques gain a precious chance to participate and reinforce social relations through their responses to social media tags, remarks or statements.

Data Analytics

Libraries will play an active part in data analytics completely. It has been a library that collects, organizes and protects precious data for a long time. Modern research and information collection has taken a long time since libraries managed and accessed some of the oldest internet dial-ups. Digital data are now so generously gathered that only analyzing the information to discover significant conclusions about the overflow of data resides as one of the greatest problems.

In the years to come, these organizations will have to decide the best way to use the information they have access to. Compile and connect information through study studies and reports. Opportunities include:

- Providing users with easy information to search and comprehensibility.
- Created content from information sources development and promotion.
- Translate information into displays and programs of information.

There is a distinctive opportunity to become part of the shift for those fascinated by the contemporary faces of today's library systems. Tomorrow, librarians can assist with a library studies degree on-line at the USC Marshall School of Business to lead fresh developments in library technology and program creation. This state-of - the-art program enables learners to learn how to form the future of world libraries.

5.1. Management of Change: Concept, Need, Impact, Strategies

For any organization, as well as the library, modification will come back from one in every of 2 sources: internal or external. Internal changes are changes initiated inside the organization and relate to the way to do things, once to try to things or what new things to try to do. The important problems here are the way to build these changes usually acceptable to or accepted by the bulk inside the organization. Thus, the difficulty of participation, manipulation and resistance become of some significance within the management of internal modification. All of those problems are ways to influence the response of people inside the organization to the changes. They are calculated to completely have an effect on the perception of the individual moreover as his attitudinal and activity disposition to the changes.

Participation entails involving those to be stricken by the modification in its formulation and implementation. In this manner it is additional doubtless to secure their commitment and general disposition to just accept the results of the modification method. However, it is recognized that democratic ways of managing modification is time intense and expensive and there could also be would like insure circumstances to use a technique of non-public power. This could be so additional applicable in things wherever there is formal, recognized and accepted authority or wherever personal power arises from the result of personal magnetism. In either case, power ways are best used wherever commitment to the changes method is not essential for its prospering implementation or wherever the resources on the market ar restricted or once very little resistance is anticipated.

Participatory ways, however, should not be confused with manipulation. Manipulation is that the aware structuring of an occurrence so others, in spite of the appearance of participation, find yourself behaving within the manner supposed by the modification agent. Manipulation might involve the utilization of inducements or hidden threats to secure compliance or weaken the temptation to resist modification. Its long success is, but continuously doubtful.

Resistance to vary should be recognized as an initial 1st reaction of the bulk of individuals. Inside a company, therefore, this could best be addressed through negotiation and therefore the modification method expedited through substance, enlightenment and education. The effectiveness of such negotiation is greatly increased by appreciating the causes of resistance. This might embrace worry of losing some current advantage of profit, a way of inadequate arising from the challenge of feat new skills, new activity pattern, new angle or new ways in which of thinking or with reference to folks. On the other hand, resistance or hostility to vary might entail a basic distinction of viewpoint and will be a health development to be used constructively. Those resisting a specific modification usually have one thing of import to mention. For this reason, the premise of their resistance ought to be adequately thought-about and created use of as applicable.

Nonetheless, it is external modification or changes within the setting during which the organization needs to operate that are usually the additional crucial ones. Changes within the setting tend to be of tremendous import and sometimes tax the artistic ability of the organization. Such changes at the best is anticipated however will seldom be controlled. And nevertheless it is from such changes that threats to the terribly survival of the organization might and do arise. Changes within the setting of a company tend to arise from one or additional of 4 sources: technological, economic, social and political.

Technological changes are either method or market driven. Within the former, new ways, processes or approaches of doing things whereas within the latter, new merchandise would possibly force on a company a modification of stress. Technology development has been the foremost potent issue creating for dramatic changes within the data world. Changes will result in turbulent or traumatic things inside any organization. The goal of modification management is therefore to modulate and contain the negative consequences of such turbulent or conflict scenario while drawing strength and renewal from the numerous opportunities that modification provides. Management of modification therefore entails correct and perceptive anticipation of such opportunities and therefore the adoption of appropriate ways to exploit them. Management might feel that it's absolutely valid reasons for introducing structure modification, as an example to retort to changes within the setting – market or technological, take care of the new arrangements needed following a purchase, merge or takeover or to eliminate overlapping areas of activity. different reasons embrace to cater for the introduction of latest activities or the elimination of recent ones, gain economies of scale by amalgamating activities, facilitate higher coordination, management or communications and to change operations to position deciding nearer to the purpose of action, to scale back the scale of an unwieldy head workplace and/ or to chop down on paperwork, centralize operations to produce for higher management from the highest, accommodate management modifications and to 'shake up the business a bit'- management are familiar to articulate a belief that change may be a input in itself. There might be some truth during this in an exceedingly stagnant organization; however 'change for change's sake' may be a dangerous belief.

Librarians and Management of Change

Librarians and data specialists' are approaching a call purpose. they need to decide whether or not they can produce changes in libraries that parallel the ever-changing desires for data in society, and therefore thrive within the electronic age, or whether or not they can still serve their ancient role because the custodians of books and alternative data media. Within the words of Dowlin (1984) "the library has historically been outlined as an area for books and therefore the bibliotheca as a keeper of books. The librarians' ties or association with books has served as associate plus. We have been able to use the romantic aura of books to colors ourselves as necessary. Yet, as society has developed alternative means that for storage and transmission of data and knowledge, our ability to impress society with our importance has shriveled, our ties to books could become a liability".

The need for organized access to data has accrued within the electronic age. A profession which will organize several books brings several of the abilities required for organizing data, no matter format. If a book is viewed as a way to associate finish – access to data – it then becomes do able to think about alternative means that to a similar finish and to incorporate these means into style. The role of librarians and data specialists these days is to extend access to information. New skills so have to be compelled to be learned. The method of adjusting libraries and data centers has started. It is time for the librarians and data specialists to tackle the task consistently.

We should develop and outline our role before others force their definition upon us. By the way to reach our definition, we have a tendency to should become attentive to have a tendency together that impact what we do currently, or can neutralize the long run. Librarians as well as data specialists have crucial roles in managing and providing access to information. The electronic library is a very important ingredient for the standard of life in future societies and libraries and librarians have the responsibility for transportation them into being. The method is not easy, it will need the mastery of the many and varied tools by people who care to satisfy the promise.

Librarians have perpetually served as guides to data resources. If the philosophy of service is to seek out the vehicle carrying the knowledge, it must be dilated. If the librarian's concern is for activity the knowledge, no matter the instrumentality, one has already created major progress towards the electronic library. Whereas the standard criterion is to seek out the instrumentality of the knowledge, the new criterion within the ICT era relies on finding the knowledge. Therefore, a librarian or data specialist who is ICT literate may be a valued skilled conjointly viewed as associate agent of knowledge transfer associated an advocate for information accessibility.

It is necessary to notice here that amendment management within the data world entails most significantly, each human and instrumentation. Human within the sense of managing the skilled angle to vary management in data provision caused by the ICT whereas change management in instrumentation involves managing the new ICT instrumentation that is step by step commutation the recent standard criterion of finding the instrumentality of data by finding the knowledge itself. Hence, the necessity to debate the management of amendment in library data resources. This includes preservation of digitized library data resources and necessities, conjointly the issues with digitization of library data resources.

Need for change in library

In order to survive and grow each organization/ library must rely upon their interaction with their external surroundings. They get input from their surroundings, rework them through numerous processes and export output to the surroundings. The management of amendment may be a complicated method that involves plenty of exercise on the part of the management of any organization or establishment and it needs extended foresight.

The following are the broad needs for management of change in library:

- Information explosion.
- Impact of Information and Communication Technology (ICT).
- Globalization.

Change is not any a lot of a matter of choice; but, it is the foremost vital obstacle to surmount by people and organizations that need to survive. Modification as a development has long been studied in art, science and humanity. However, the revived interest, that the topic has attracted in recent times, seems to own return from the eminent application of distilled rules in evolution to organizational/library management.

5.2. STRESS MANAGEMENT

Stress is extremely tough because it could be a reaction by us to completely vary state of affairs otherwise and so the stresses of various folks area unit different from one another we have a tendency to cannot outline it generally. The strain that i am having is not a stress the least bit to a different person and vise-versa.

When library skilled face the case he/she cannot handle, they feel stressed. Even after them area unit weighed down or overworked, and then additionally they feel wired.

Stress is that the state of affairs from that we wish to come back out. We have a tendency to can-not keep in this state of affairs for an extended time. We would like relief from it.

"Stress usually outlined as response to concrete or mentally evoked threats to a person's bodily equilibrium (Levine, 2005). Dislike stress responses occur once someone fails to retort effectively to mental, emotional, or physical demands (Bansal & Yadav, 2010). These threats are often real or notional. From a protagonist perspective, stress is a survival mechanism to evoke physiological changes required to flee a threat (Levine, 2005). However, issues might arise once money, family, or geographical point stress induces the same response".

According to Merriam-Webster lexicon, "Stress could be a constrictive force or influence. It is a force exerted once one body or part presses on, pulls or, pushes against, or tends to compress or twist another body or body part; a physical chemical or emotional issue that causes bodily or mental tension and will be an element in wellness causation".

Research has found that the degree of stress that an individual encounters has been connected to a person's physical health, the strength of their social relationship, their employment or commitments, and traumatic events (Sprague, Verona, Kalkhoff & Kilmer, 2011). Likelihood is you will be able to think about somebody who remains calm despite a crunching employment, or reports stress although they need restricted responsibilities. One rationalization is that we have a tendency to develop our own stress schema (Lazarus, 1999) i.e. stress pattern in different language. This is a mental illustration of stress and what constitutes as a nerve-racking event. This means that that an event is solely as nerve-racking as perceived by a personal. However, commonalities area unit found between library professionals and also the events that elicit a robust stress response.

Negative stress causes malady among the body and Positive / sensible stress feeds our creative thinking and motivates us to realize a lot of.

Excessive stress can affect a librarian's health by:

A. Reducing productivity

B. Contribution to premature ageing

C. Worsening current health issues

Stress Pattern : Stress Pattern is thought as experiencing one or a lot of the physical and emotional symptoms and behavior patterns like quicker pulse rate, Muscle tension, inflated pressure, Knots in abdomen or tightness within the space, Anxious, expanded pupils, Dry mouth, Fatigue, Tension within the neck or shoulder muscles, Chest pain, Not proper sleep, symptom, constipation, or diarrhea, Lack of concentration,

Frustrated, Worrying regarding things not governable, Procrastination etc.. . To best management your stress, it is wise begin by being awake to your own symptoms.

Stressors : Stressor is an occasion, event or amendment wherever we tend to want we tend to cannot cope. Since this demand might consume tangible physical and mental resources, it will produce stress and mayhem in librarian's lives. Stress is divided into 2 categories: Internal & External.

Internal : Mental and Emotional stressors:

Public Speaking : For many librarians address could be a mental and emotional agent. Presenting ahead of an audience could be a mental agent not solely to the library professionals however to the lecturers additionally in several cases. Librarian does not have observed of speaking on the stage like lecturers. Provided that task, performance is needed. This provides a logical clarification as address being according as a considerably stressful event.

Tension : Librarian can take tension of the situation he/she is facing, and be stressful.

Interpretation : Stress is not caused by the event or scenario itself, however it caused on however we tend to interpret it and there are many varieties of priorities of librarians, several among which may interpret the things wrong and might take stress.

Perfection : Librarians, who are compulsive, could also be a lot of nerve-wracking than others. They will take stress due to their smallest mistake.

External :

Environmental Stressors : Environmental stressors might embrace crowd within the library, noise within the library, or maybe traffic jam of the library software system, library employees operating with different departments of the college.

Social / Job Stressors : Job stressors will embrace human interaction and communication within the college, negative or hurtful things employees or colleagues might enlighten you and even happy events like obtaining sensible pay or publication a paper or obtaining a degree or maybe obtaining calls as a V. C. campaigner as a topic skilled will all contribute to fret levels. Demands for everyday living will become stressors within the lifetime of librarian like ordering the books on time, process the books at intervals the deadlines and even workplace politics will all contribute to those symptoms. In several cases librarian is younger than the opposite library employees. This could even be an agent. He/she needs to handle them, teach new trends to them will become an agent.

New technology could be a huge example of a agent these days for librarians. If he/she is not curious about learning the advancements in technology then he/she will face issues.

Behavioral : Procrastination and ways in which to avoid it: Procrastination refers to the act of replacement high-priority actions with task of low-priority and therefore pushing aside necessary tasks to a later time. It will actually cause undue stress and even depression in one's life, if left un-dealt with. There are 100 of many reasons why folks procrastinate such as being unorganized and not having skills to finish tasks, feeling a concern of failing or rejection at work.

Following are the two ways to avoid procrastination:

1. Breaking down tasks into smaller units one issue at a time. Each massive work has tiny parts or tasks to try to do. After we split the work into tiny things, it is simple to handle the quality of it.
2. Keeping a diary to assist keep a track of due dates of our next approaching tasks. After, we write down the little elements of the large work and priorities

the little tasks. We have a tendency to feel that there is nothing to require tension. Therefore we will simply complete the work before its due time or before the point.

Preventing Stress

- Deep respiratory, relaxation, and meditation: Our overall health and well-being. Even this implies setting aside twenty minutes each day for ourselves, it is extraordinarily worthy for us to do therefore. Focusing our mind, thoughts, breathing, and our overall body posture permits us to completely relax physically, mentally, and showing emotion.
- *Nutritious diet*: A poor diet will lead United States to feeling mentally and physically drained. It will subsume our emotional level, therefore making a lot of stress in our life. However, after we are uptake well and experiencing adequate nutrition, our energetic body are ready to manage more stressors and that we are more attentive to handle them. Stimulants like alkaloid, tobacco, and alcohol will exacerbate stress responses therefore though we have a tendency to could also be tempted to show to those habits to manage our stress, it is definitely potential they will increase our stress levels further.
- *Exercise* : Negative feeling and emotions typically accompanies stress. Once we have a tendency to have feelings of concern, sadness, anxiety, or anger, stress typically accompanies these emotions. Exercise will facilitate us to stimulate these feelings and provides us the energy to tackle our daily tasks. If we have a tendency to do not presently have a daily exercise regime, i challenge to make one for ourselves even if it is simply a couple of moments every day. We will do things as straightforward as a couple of yoga postures, sit-ups, or perhaps push-ups to stimulate the endorphins exaggerated

through exercise that helps United States to feel happy and revived.

- *Organized* : once we have a tendency to measure unorganized in our work and home lives we have a tendency to become unbalanced physically, showing emotion, and mentally. Once things do not have a home of their own, then your belongings become scattered and unfocused. Turning into a lot of organized and prioritizing each our work and home life greatly enhances our energy and reduces our stress level.
- *Being Prepared* : If we all know that a trying event is arising in our life, follow and inure it. If we have a tendency to feel a trying scenario with a coworker, loved one or friend take a deep breath, relax, and start once more. Restful our body, taking a couple of breaths, and start speaking in an exceedingly heat, pleasant manner instead of yelling or raising your voice. Advance preparation for trying events can assist you manages matters higher within the long run.
- *Positive attitude* : Things that happen in your life typically times looks like disasters. Rather than viewing them as therefore, read things as opportunities and learning experiences and do not allow them to get you down. Take a deep breath, relax, center your thoughts, and maintain a positive perspective. What you channelize to universe comes back to you. Once trying things occur in your life, channelize positive vibes of energy and also the same can come to you. Facing and Accepting difficult situation: Learning to accept the situation rather than worry and stress about it. Face the difficult situation head-on with positivity and we will find the answers we seek in an easy way.
- *Facing and acceptive troublesome situation*: Learning

to just accept matters instead of worry and stress regarding it. Face the troublesome scenario head-on with positivism and we have a tendency to notice the answers we look for in a straightforward means.

- *Balance between work and personal life* : interact in activities that may relax our body and facilitate and helps to ignore our worries. This might be a fun twenty minute session of game twiddling with our family, observance a picture show, taking a walk, riding a bicycle, or even taking a soothing tub. Finding balance in your life makes a stress-free setting for yourself.
- *Social support* : Stress is usually worsened after we have not any outlet or means that of discussing our problems. Create time to socialize and keep in grips along with your family and friends. If you are feeling powerless, seek advice from somebody us you will trust. Generally merely talking regarding your feelings will offer you revived strength to tackle your goals.
- *Hired maid/ Cook at home* : Hiring a Maid / Cook may be a sensible resolution for population chores. Schedule yourself some free time every day; even it is just for a couple of minutes. You will notice by reflective and restful mediate the chores; we are going to have a lot of energy to complete what is required. Cook will not be appreciated reception by family generally; then again a minimum of hiring an Assistant for preparation chores may be a stronger resolution.

This will facilitate us to require charge of our mind, body and spirit in ways in which can permit us to disembarrass the self of stress whereas encouraging a deeper sense of peace and well-being.

Stress Coping Skills / Healing Ways

There are five different types of coping skills to deal with stressors in our life.

- Physical stress brick includes healthy mode and adequate sleep. As a stress brick strategy we have to go to bed early in order that once awake we have a tendency to feel recent as we have a tendency to get relaxed entirely. We have to eat meals at regular times & do less snacking in between meals. Having a healthy diet and taking a victuals supplements if required. Additional we will add quiet, taking a nap, taking a heat bath, burning scented candles or obtaining a massage to our stress coping physical methods. Keeping the list prepared for coping. We will conjointly add here going for a picnic.
- *Emotional* : Building our own vanity, confidence, dotty our self-image can have an effect on in our emotional we have a tendency to be good and if we have a tendency to have positive in our mind we are relax and additional progress with others.
- *Social* : Building positive relationships embody the coping skills. once we build smart and healthy relationship with our colleagues, relatives, friends, and neighbors, we will become relaxed simply in our stressful events by the support we have a tendency to get from them.
- *Mental skills* : It includes journaling, renewal, and rest: Author found Journaling could be an excellent technique. Author won't to write a journal when wedding. She found it absolutely was very strengthening her system. She conjointly feels that the issues faced by her will have answers & positive meanings in it once we assume right. And whereas journaling we actually assume right, therefore this is often an awfully smart habit for managing stress.
- Spirituality means that to the author "having

complete religion on the ability, whom we will decision GOD essentially, and having total quality on 'He handles my life things and no matter can happen in my life, can happen simply to improve myself' and every one the obstacles are learning experiences and zip negative will happen in my life, once I have a robust support of my dotty GOD." Therefore meditation, prayer, spirituality and conjointly daily Saadhanaa or Upaasanaa helps a heap to deal with the unwanted stress of our daily life. Prayer ought to be done from all-time low of our heart, all the cell in our body at the same time ought to pray to GOD. This system is extremely very powerful. The author has several smart experiences of this.

- Getting into the non-secular swing of things is not any simple matter for the common person. While not Spirituality the adverse thoughts of doubt and worry surge from the subconscious. They are the "army of the aliens" that should be place to flight. This explains why it is therefore typically, "darkest before the dawn".

Library Professionals area unit extremely stressed in gift state of affairs. There are many various kinds of issues the Library Professionals need to face at this hour. No matter is that the cause, he / she need to usually handle the matter alone. This profession is in question repeatedly. Within the educational setup it is seen that there are several disparities concerning this profession additionally as these professionals. No one is coming back forward to resolve the issues of the Library Professionals.

5.3. TIME MANAGEMENT

Managing a library presents distinctive time challenges to the professionals concerned. Libraries are service-oriented establishments and therefore the majority of their shoppers are "drop-ins" that creates problems with time management that are less problematic in different skilled things wherever time and shoppers are regular. These time challenges will increase frustration and reduce job satisfaction. Selecting acceptable time management ways, however, will enhance professionals' lives by increasing work productivity, bolstering shallowness, and making longer for private pursuits. A method of increasing time management skills is to look at the analysis and literature to uncover common themes. By viewing however librarians in numerous settings pay their time and therefore the activities they describe as time wasters, it is doable to recommend advantageous time management ways. There are a mess of techniques offered, therefore librarians should analyze their own environments and examine their personal preferences to decide on the foremost acceptable ways.

These are 2 principles are essential to the appliance of your time management ways. so as to maximize their time, librarians should rank the foremost vital tasks, and complete them in an exceedingly timely manner.

The Importance of Time Management

Increasing technological and informational demands, not to mention decreasing budget and personnel allowances, emphasizes the importance of utilizing time management skills: "Public directors throughout the country are combating a standard dilemma: however will public libraries deliver services a lot of expeditiously and effectively with no increase - and in several cases a decrease - in spending?" (Samuelson, 1981). The solution to the current quandary is time management. Individuals and organizations might accomplish a lot of within the same quantity of your time if they eliminated time wasters and increased productivity. As an example, one study has shown that the common yank employee wastes forty five percentages of the day (Gothberg & Riggs, 1988). This result could seem onerous to believe, however if researchers are able to determine this important proportion of wasted time, organizations got to examine however their personnel are defrayment their time so as to channel these individuals into a lot of productive activities. what is more, even if managers area unit upset regarding the increasing demands placed on them, they do not appear to be taking full advantage of the time resources they are have: "Many library managers are frustrated by the very fact that a lot of associated a lot of demands are being placed on what seems to them as an already crowded schedule.

Many directors could feel this stress as a result of they are doing not manage their time well" (Leach, 1980). If librarians makes scope of your time management methods like setting goals, delegation and prioritizing, they will be higher able to handle these increasing demands.

Time management offers edges to each people and organizations. Individual's expertise increased vanity and a bigger feeling of management over their time, whereas organizations like increased productivity and higher services: "Taking positive action toward managing library time challenges will result in increased feelings of self-worth and vanity. It may result in a stronger library program that meets the present and future desires of users" (Walster, 1993). This self-reinforcing cycle will result in a win-win scenario for all parties concerned. So as to balance conflicting demands and profit of the advantages of your time management, librarians should become a lot of economical and effective at what they are doing. Though it should not be realistic to assume that librarians will ever accomplish everything they would ideally prefer to do, correct time management will facilitate them determine priorities, delegate responsibility and manage the library in an exceedingly manner that may maximize the restricted time offered.

Time Management Strategies

Covey (1989), though not a librarian, presents a helpful framework for examining time management. He asserts that folks ought to be proactive and think about necessary activities they will influence or amendment. The primary step is for people to form personal mission statements:

Once you have got that sense of mission, you have got the essence of your own proactivity. you have got the vision and also the values that direct your life. You have got the essential direction from that you set your long-term and short-term. you have got the facility of a written constitution supported correct principles, against which each call regarding the foremost effective use of it slow, your abilities, and your energies is effectively measured. This mission statement could be a central part of your time management and provides folks a broad perspective that enables them to pick their priorities. Keeping these priorities in mind and coming up with around them, helps folks accomplish the items in their lives that are the foremost necessary to them. So as to spot however folks pay their time and the way they get sidetracked from their most vital activities, Covey establishes a matrix with four quadrants.

Quadrant I important/urgent	Quadrant II important/not urgent
Quadrant III not important/urgent	Quadrant IV not important/not urgent

Fig. 1.

Source **: https://www.bishophouse.com/wp-content/uploads/2013/02/Effective-Perscnal-Management-with-Covey-The-4-Quads.pdf**

According to Covey, many folks pay an excessive amount of time in Quadrant I that reinforces a crisis mentality. Others pay an excessive amount of time in Quadrant III as a result of the incorrectly assume these imperative problems are necessary.

Many people use Quadrant IV as associate degree escape as a result of these activities ar neither imperative or necessary, they have an inclination to be simple. the most effective place, in line with Covey, for folks to pay the bulk of their time is Quadrant II as a result of these ar the effective, necessary activities that replicate people's priorities: The target of Quadrant II management is to manage our lives effectively - from a middle of sound principles, from a data of our personal mission, with a spotlight on the necessary likewise because the imperative, and among the framework of maintaining a balance between increasing our production and increasing our production capability.

Focusing on Quadrant II empowers folks to pay time on necessary and effective activities. It conjointly allows folks to balance their lives around activities that are meaningful and gratifying for them. Once folks create an acutely aware effort to incorporate these necessary goals in their schedules, they are victimization their time well.

Covey's paradigm is a necessary time management tool that is particularly helpful for establishing priorities and making a satisfying balance of important activities. The importance of creating priorities and goals is often mentioned within the time management literature. For instance, Cochran (1992) emphasizes the importance of goal-setting as a primary step in effective time use: "The start in any effective time management program involves distinctive personal and skilled values and establishing goals and objectives in support of these values. All else in effective time management stems from this process". Having a mission statement, establishing goals, and coming up with supported personal priorities will facilitate folks create selections to effectively manage their time.

Once priorities are established, it is helpful to look at individual ways that may alleviate specific time management issues. For instance, time spent in conferences is one in every of the foremost frequent time wasters cited within the analysis literature. There are pointers, however, that may facilitate verify once conferences are necessary and there are ways for making things wherever conferences are run as with efficiency and effectively as doable. Hawkins (1989) provides helpful ways for keeping conferences on task: provide the team advance notice of topics to be mentioned in problem-solving or decision-making sessions. Do not underestimate the worth of "thought time" for team members before being asked to comment or act on that avoid distractions throughout team problem-solving or decision-making sessions.

Planning ahead, informing others of the agenda, and keeping the meeting targeted will scale back the number of your time spent in conferences whereas increasing their potential productivity. Raney (1988) shares an analogous philosophy with regard to coming up with for meetings: Run the meeting effectively: distribute the agenda prior to time; let members recognize before what input they are going to be asked to produce at the meeting; begin and endways time; target agenda items; remain target; set time and purpose for consecutive meeting, and write minutes right away.

Carefully managing conferences through the notice of your time wasters will save valuable time while not a loss within the flow of information: "with correct preparation and leadership, several conferences will move quickly and still come through their purpose, or need not be known as at all" (Mauro & Weber, 1980). Adopting these suggestions will limit the amount of conferences, likewise because the folks directly concerned in every meeting, and keep the content of the meeting targeted and productive so maximizing the employment of this point for all personnel concerned. Authorization is in our own way to form longer for skilled activities that need the abilities of a trained librarian by distribution alternative tasks to applicable employee's members. It addresses the matter of 'attempting an excessive amount of promptly and estimating time unrealistically' by decreasing the amount of tasks a manager makes an attempt individually:

Effectively authorization to others is probably the only most powerful high-leverage activity there is. Transferring responsibility to alternative skillful and trained folks allows you to allow your energies to alternative high-leverage activities. Delegation means that growth, each for people and for organizations. (Covey, 1989)

Delegation will profit all parties concerned. It permits the manager to attend to high priority things, it will increase the potency of the organization, and it reinforces subordinates by utilizing their skills to their fullest capacity:

"Not solely will delegation free the manager to pursue alternative tasks him/herself, delegation could be a powerful tool for private and skilled growth for subordinates" (Hawk,ns, 1989). Subordinates get a chance for growth and learning from their raised responsibility, and professionals have longer to accomplish the desired tasks that they were trained. Additionally to distribution tasks at the foremost applicable level, delegation can even be accustomed manage interruptions like phone calls and drop-in guests. Cochran (1992) suggests that if managers will designate somebody to answer the phone and screen guests, several of those interruptions is decreased or rescheduled at applicable times.

Delegation could be a powerful tool that addresses many common time management issues. Managers have to be compelled to examine problems that will be keeping them from authorization responsibility effectively and commit themselves to distribution responsibility to others so as to manage their own valuable time a lot of sagely.

There are many alternative time management ways obtainable that address problems like handling paper, managing crises, and organizing the physical setting. The particular ways chosen ought to replicate the individual's mission statement, priorities, goals, and distinctive time chal'enges. Time management is a personal alternative of applicable strategies: "to be effective, time management should be personal. That is, librarians should adopt and adapt the recommended techniques to suit their own things. No specific methodology or technique works universally" (Cochran, 1992). Not solely can completely different ways apply to different folks, however time management could be a method that must be flexible to ever-changing things at totally different points in time. Because of the knowledge explosion and ever ever-changing technologies, librarians have to be compelled to be ready to regulate their ways to accommodate change: "Librarians add a volatile and ever-changing setting. It is necessary to possess selections and techniques that may be applied to new and totally different things. One size does not match bushed time management for librarians (Walster, 1993). The ways mentioned here represent solely a sampling of doable techniques for effectively managing time. Though librarians have common time issues, these ways solely function general pointers every librarian is exclusive and wishes to make your mind up that strategies can maximize his or her use of your time.

Librarians pay their time and therefore the activities they contemplate time wasters have disclosed many areas wherever the appliance of your time management ways will increase the potency and effectiveness of library management.

Contemplate time wasters have disclosed many areas wherever the appliance of your time management ways will increase the potency and effectiveness of library management.

5.4. PROJECT MANAGEMENT

The study of project management (PM) began with the work of Frederick Taylor, who is attributable with the event of the conception of scientific management, which involves the applying of the mathematical study of the varied parts of the processes concerned within the work of organizations. As Taylor's work began in manufacturing operations, project management has its origins within the producing sector, as well. Currently, project management is employed in varied segments of the company sector, primarily in production operations, however in some aspects of service industries, also as data technology. Additionally, the employment of PM software package to arrange and track comes is changing into additional widespread. Project management has been employed in the general public sector, as well, together with in libraries.

With relevance library and data services, the main target on project management has associated with problems like renovation, design, and building comes for branding new and enlarged library facilities and IT system migration and implementation, also as smaller comes. It is vital to notice that in support and documentation of labor in libraries, there has been restricted provision of knowledge associated with project management in libraries within the LIS literature. Thus, in providing a framework for the discussion of project management in libraries, the discussion can embrace the employment of project management within the personal and public sectors, with a selected specialize in producing, wherever the study of project management began, and data technology, that relates thus closely to library and data services. The applying of project management techniques in libraries are going to be self-addressed, as can the literature of project management, that documents and supports add organizations.

Project Management in Libraries

In libraries, PM principles are applicable in regard to several organization-wide and unit-specific activities, like style and building comes for brand spanking new and enlarged library facilities and therefore the implementation of and migration to new integrated library data systems. There is restricted literature that addresses project management of such building comes, grant funding to support PM programs, and a few thought of the management of individual comes. specially, the successful use of project management in library applications has been addressed within the literature, with a spotlight on serving to library managers to structure tasks and notice the proper individuals to finish them, whereas measure the success of the comes. There is recent mention of exploitation project management techniques to assist managers who administrate several comes quickly. One such example is that of Lois Langer, the coordination professional at Hennepin County Library and therefore the principal professional at Eden grassland Library, each in Gopher State. In managing multiple comes quickly, Langer has known project management tools as important for coordinative many skilled comes, however conjointly personal projects.

With reference to the restricted in-house data of PM principles and practices in several libraries, the Rural Library Project within the USA provides project management support to little rural libraries. The initial work of the Rural Library Project, exploitation project management to make new libraries in rural communities, met with nice success. The Rural Library Project has conjointly enforced coaching programs for the employees of libraries8 and represents an example of steerage and help as libraries begin to use project management methodologies.

CONCLUSION

As project management has been a great tool within the non-public sector; it is possible that in libraries project management are going to be used on a bigger scale. the various package applications may be integrated into most coming up with systems and every one offer coaching to boost the performance of project managers. Although libraries never totally use project management throughout structure operations, the primary steps within the method, like the design and initiation phases are useful and will be used as a guide to produce an economical work setting. so as to make sure the foremost economical and effective use of resources and therefore the completion of comes that contribute to overall structure performance, it is necessary to produce applicable support for those that have project management responsibilities.

REVIEW QUESTIONS

1. Explain the establishment of development of libraries in India.
2. Describe the Stress Management in library.
3. Describe the Time Management in library.
4. Describe the Project Management and the importance in library.

References

- "Emotion & Behavior Lab Verona - Psychology Department Labs." 2012.
- "Merriam-Webster Online: Dictionary and Thesaurus." 2003.
- "Stress and Emotion: A New Synthesis - Richard S ... - Google Books." 2011.
- "The Game of Life and How to Play It by Florence Scovell Shinn." 2007. *http://www.sacred-texts.com/nth/shinn/gol/*
- "Reprogramming Yourself" By Rev. La Vonda Young, Divine Blessings Academy, USA.
- Adeyoyin, Samuel Olu; Imam, Abayomi; and Bello, Taofik Olatunde, "Management of Change in the 21st Century Libraries and Information Centers" (2012). Library Philosophy and Practice (e-journal). 695. *http://digitalcommons.unl.edu/libphilprac/695*
- Aguolu C. C. , Aguolu I. E. 2002 Library and information management in Nigeria Ed-Linform Services Maiduguri, Nigeria
- Anthony, William P. (1993). "Strategic Human Resource Management", Dryden Press, New York.
- Application of total quality management to library and Information services in indian open universities, Dr.G. Saroja www.col.org/forum/pcfpapers/saroja.pdf
- Berner, A. (1987). The importance of time management in the small library. Special Libraries, 78(4), 271-276.
- Bernhardt, K. L., Donthu, N., & Kennett, P.A. A longitudinal analysis of satisfaction and profitability. Journal of Business Research, 2000, 47, 161-171.

- Besterfield, D.H. Total Quality Management. New Jersey: Prentice Hall Incorporation. 1999.
- Blackburn R. , Rosen B. 1993 Total quality and human resources management: Lessons learned from Baldrige award winning companies The Academy of Management Executives 7 (3) 49 - 66
- Blackburn, R., & Rosen, B. (1993). Total quality and human resources management: lessons learned from Baldrige award-winning companies. The Academy of Management Executive, 7(3), 49-66.
- Braham J. 1989 Money talks Industry Week 17 23 -
- Brandt, D. R. Linking measures of customer satisfaction, value, and loyalty to market and financial performance: Basic methods and key considerations. In Proceedings of ASQ's 54th Annual Quality Congress.2000, Milwaukee, Wis.: ASQ Quality.
- Broyles, Jack, [et al.] eds. (1983). Financial Management Handbook, 2 ed. England: Gower.
- Bryson, John. (1990). Effective Library and Information Center Management. England: Gower. Evan, G Edward. (1976). Management Techniques for Libraries. New York:'Academic press.
- Buzzell, R. & Gale, B. The PIMS principles: Linking strategy to performance, New York: Free Press. 1997.
- C. C. Yee and Y. Y. Chen, "Performance appraisal system using multifactorial evaluation Model", PWASET, vol. 41, pp 231-235, 2009.
- Cascio W. F. 1987 Do good or poor performers leave? A meta-analysis of the relationship between performance and turnover The Academy of Management Journal 30 (4) 744 - 762 DOI : 10.2307/256158
- Cavaleri S. , Obloj K. 1993 Management system: A global perspective Wadsworth Belmont, CA
- Chand, S. (2015). Human resource planning: Objectives, Need, Importance and Levels. Retrieved: 26th November, 2015. From: http:// *www.humanresourceplanningobjective/ needs,importance,andlevels.htm*
- Choi, T. Y., & Eboch, K. The TQM paradox: Relations among TQM practices, plant performance, and customer satisfaction. Journal of Operations Management, 1998, 17,

(1), 59-75.

- Cochran, J. W. (1992) Time management handbook for librarians. New York: Greenwood Press.
- Concept of quality in library services: an overview
- Covey, S. R. (1989). The seven habits of highly effective people: Restoring the character ethic. New York: Simon & Schuster.
- Curkovic, S., Vickery, S. K., & Droge, C. Quality and business performance: An empirical study of first-tier automotive suppliers. Quality Management Journal, 1999, 6 (2), 29-40.
- Dale, B. G., Van Der Wiele, T., & Van Iwaarden, J. (2013). Managing quality. John Wiley & Sons.
- Deming W.E. Out of the Crisis. MIT Press, Cambridge, MA.1995.
- Dow, D., Samson, D., & Ford, S. Exploding the myth: Do all quality management practices contribute to superior quality performance? Production and Operations Management, 1999, 8 (1), 1-27.
- Dr. Jaspal S. Sandhu , Secretary , University Grants Commission ; Ministry of Human resource Development . (28 July 2014)
- Drucker P. 1954 The practice of management Harper & Row New York
- E. N. Makokha, G. Namusonge, C. Kanali, and A. C. Milgo, "Determinants of effectiveness of employee performance appraisal system in institution of higher learning: a survey of public universities in Nakuru County, European journal of business and management, vol. 6, no. 8, 2014.
- Easton, G. S. & Jarrell, S. L. The effects of total quality management on corporate performance: An empirical investigation, The Journal of Business, 1998, 71(2), 253-308.
- Edoka B. E. 2000 Introduction to library science Palma Publishing & Links Coy Onitsha, Nigeria
- Edvardsson, B., Johnson, M. D., Gustafsson, A., & Strandvik, T. The effects of satisfaction and loyalty on profits and growth: Products versus services. Total Quality Management, 2000, 11 (7), 917-927.
- Everhart, N. (1994). How high school library media specialists in automated and non-automated media centers spend their

time: Implications for library media educators. Journal of Education for Library and Information Science, 35(1), 3-19.

- F. F. Asamu, "Perception of performance appraisal and workers' performance in Wema bank headquarters", Lagos, Global Journal of Arts, Humanities and Social Sciences, vol. 1, no. 4, pp. 89-101, 2013.
- Fayol H., Coubrough J. A. 1930 Industrial and general administration Sir Isaac Pitman & Sons London
- Fayol H. , Storrs C. 1949 General and industrial management Sir Isaac Pitman & Sons London
- Fayol H. 1917 Administrat·on industrielle et générale; prévoyance, organisation, commandement, coordination, controle H. Dunod & E. Pinat Paris
- Fisher, K., Rayner, S. & Belgrad, W. Total quality control. ASQC Quality. 1993.
- Garvin, D. A. Managing quality: The strategic and competitive edge. New York. 1991.
- George Bohlander (2002). "Managing Human Resources", Therson, p. 24.
- Gothberg, H. M. (1991a). Time management in public libraries: A study of public libraries. Public Libraries, 30(6), 350-357.
- Gothberg, H. M. (1991b). Time management in special libraries. Special Libraries, 82(2), 119-130.
- Gothberg, H. M. (1991c). Time management in state libraries. Special Libraries, 82(4), 257-266.
- Gothberg, H. M., & Riggs, D. E. (1988). Time management in academic libraries. College & Research Libraries, 49(2), 131-140.
- Government of India, Ministry of Finance (Dept. of Expenditure) O.M. No. F.23(7)-E- II(A)/83 dt. 7.2.84 and Dept. of Supply U.O.No. I.D.No.P III- 3(5)/82 dt. 17.1.83 and C.A.G's U.O.No. 1964-TA.II/21-83 dt. 23 .12.83.
- Hackman, J. R., & Wageman, R. (1995). Total quality management: empirical, conceptual, and practical issues. Administrative science quarterly, 309-342.
- Harish Chandra, Swamy, P. N., Sharada Raman, and N. Jagadeesan. "Digital Initiatives with Special Reference to Library Membership Records at the Central Library of Indian Institute of Technology, Madras". National Conventional on

Library and Information Networking (NACLIN 2000), Chennai: Papers. Ed. H K Kaul and Harish Chandra.

- Hawkins, K. W. (1989). Implementing team management in the modern library. Library Administration & Management, 4(1), 11-15.
- Heathfield, S. M. (2010). Human resources About.com *http://humanresource.about.com/od/glassary/f/whathr.htm*
- Hendricks, K. B. & Singhal, R. V. Does implementing an effective TQM program actually improve operating performance? Empirical evidence from firms that have won quality awards. Management Science, 1997, 43 (9), 1258-1274.
- Hinterhuber H. H. , Popp W. 1992 Are you a strategist or just a manager? Harvard Business Review 105 - 113
- Hinton, T. & Schaffer, R. Successful change programs begin with results, Harvard Business Review, 1994, July, pp 80-89.
- http://crln.acrl.org/content/71/6/286.short (6 August 2014)
- http://en.wikipedia.org/wiki/List of/ content management/ system (5 Aug 2014)
- http://searchsoa.techtarget.com/definition/content management system (31July 2014)
- http://sustainablecollections.com/library-space-planning. (5 Aug 2014)
- http://www.bdcnetwork.com/12-major-trends-library.(5Aug.2014)
- http://www.design0.http://site.ebrary.com/lib/inflibnet/docDetail.action. (6 August 2014)
- http://www.libraries.wright.edu/noshelfrequired/2013/12/10/e-content-in-libraries-2013;
- *https://courses.lumenlearning.com/boundless-management/chapter/bureaucratic-and-quality-control-tools-and-techniques/*
- Idih E. , Njoku J. , Idih C. 2011 Business communication for office managers Tropical Publishers Owerri, Nigeria
- Ifidon S. E. , Ifidon E. 2007 New directions in African library management Spectrum Publishers Ibadan, Nigeria
- Ifidon S. E. 1979 Participatory management in libraries

Bendel Library Journal 2 (1) 1 - 10

- Ifidon S. E. 1985 Essentials of management for African university libraries Libriservice Lagos, Nigeria
- Imaga E. U. U. 2001 Elements of management and culture in organizational behaviour Rhyee Kerex Publishers Enugu, Nigeria
- Information Solutions Group. Managing Records as the Basis for Effective Service Delivery and Public Accountability in Development. July 2000. Web. 12 May 2013. <http://siteresources.worldbank. org/EXTARCHIVES/Resources/Core%20Principles.pdf>.
- ir.inflibnet.ac.in/dxml/bitstream/handle/1944 /1370/46.pdf?
- Iwueke O. C. , Oparaku U. D. 2011 Management Classic Business Services Owerri
- J. M. Reitz, Online Dictionary for Library and Information Science (ODLIS), 2014 [Online] Copyright © 2004-2014 Availble: *http://www.abc*-clio.com/ODLIS/odlis_about.aspx (June, 10, 2014)
- J. Okpe, "Annual Performance Appraisal of Practicing Librarians: A Study of Academic Institutions in Nigeria", Arabian Journal of Business and Management Review (OMAN Chapter), vol. 2, no. 5, pp. 10-19, 2012.
- Jaffery, A. Mello (2003). "Strategic Human Resource Management", Thomson.
- Jagdish Arora & P. Prakash, New Initiatives of INFLIBNET for higher education community
- Jeevan V.K.J. Digital libraries, Ess Ess Publication, New Delhi, 2003, 236-42.
- Jenda, C. A. (1994). Management of professional time and multiple responsibilities in a subject-centered academic library. Library Administration & Management, 8(2), 97-108.
- Kent, Allen and Lancour, Harold eds. (1970). Encyclopaedia of Library and Information Science. Vol. 3. New York: Marcel Dekker, pp. 430-440.
- Khan, "Performance Appraisal's Relation with Productivity and Job Satisfaction", Journal of Managerial Sciences, vol. 1, no. 2, 2007.
- Khan, M.A. ed. (2002). Preparation and Training of library staff. India: Cosmo Publication, 70p.

- Kirti Singh, Research Scholor, J.J.T.University, Jhujunjhunu,Total Quality Management To Library And Information Services In Indian Open Universities, Journal of Business Management & Social Sciences Research (JBM&SSR) ,Volume 2, No.6, June 2013. ISSN No: 2319-5614
- K-R, Kont, and S. Jantson, "Library employees' attitudes towards the measurement and appraisal of their work performance: Study in Estonian university libraries", Library Management, vol, 34, no. 6/7, pp. 521–537, 2013.
- L.D Mangi, and Gupta S, " Human resources activities in libraries and information centers in India: a study of some apex bodies," University news, Vol. 52 (35/36), pp. 19-21, 2014.
- Langer, Lois. "Project Management Done Here." Library Journal 129, (2004): 44
- Lanka: the Author publication, vol. 2, no. 12, pp.170-183, 2002
- Leach, R. G. (1980). Finding time you never knew you had. Journal of Academic Librarianship, 6(1), 4-8.
- Magjuka R. F. Survey: Self-managed teams achieve continuous improvement best National Productivity Review (Spring) 203 - 211
- Mauro, E. H., & Weber, D. C. (1980). Time management for library staff. Journal of Library Administration, 1(4), 13-20.
- Mayo E. 1933 The human problem of industrial civilization Harvard University Press Cambridge, MA
- McGregor D. 1960 The human side of enterprise McGraw-Hill New York
- Mintzberg H. 1973 The nature of managerial work Harper & Row New York
- Mittal, R. L. (1984). Library Administration: Theory and Practice, 5th ed. Delhi: Metropolitan Book Co. Moore, Russell F ed. AMA management handbook. New York: AMA, 1970 Newton, Jack B. " Budgeting for supervisors" . In: Mali, Paul ed. Management handbook: operating guidelines, techniques and practices. New York: John Wiley and Sons, 1981, p1313-1328.
- Mittal, R.L. Library Administration: Theory and Practice. Delhi: Metropolitan, 1984. Print.

- Molnar, D., Wagner, D.A. (2004). Privacy and security in library RFID: Issues, practices and architectures. Retrieved from *http://www.cs.berkeley.edu/~dmolnar/library.pdf*
- Mostafa Moballeghi and B. Shivaraj. Why TQM Initiatives fails? The ICFAI Journal of Operations Management, Vol.4, No.4, 2006 November, pp.65-74.
- Mostafa Moballeghi. Total Quality Management (TQM) in Practice, SCMS Journal of Indian Management, Vol.4, No.3, 2007 July-September, pp. 67-73.
- Muchinsky. A quality system for education. Wisconsin, ASQC Quality Press. 1993.
- National Institute of Science and Technology (NIST). Baldrige quality award program, criteria for performance excellence, Washington, D.C.: National Institute of Standards and Technology. 2000.
- Naumann, E., & Hoisington, S. H. Customer centered Six Sigma. Milwaukee, Wis.: ASQ Quality. 2000.
- Netaji Subhas Open University (2007). MLIS-E3 course materials: Academic Library System. Kolkata: 28-30p.
- New Delhi: DELNET, 2001: 37-51. Print.
- News,48(07)February 15-21, 2010, 4-13 .
- Nimai Chand Saha, Koushik Ghosh, Tapas Mondal,"Training & Development Of Library Professionals For It Application In University Libraries: An Overview", 5th Convention PLANNER -2007, Gauhati University,Guwahati, December 7-8, 2007
- Nnadozie C. O. 2007 Foundations of library practice Springfield Publishers Owerri, Nigeria
- Norreklit, H. The balance on the balanced scorecard—A critical analysis of some of its assumptions. Management Accounting Research 11, 2000, pp.65-88.
- Nwachukwu C. C. 1988 Management: Theory and practice Africana-Feb Publishers Ibadan, Nigeria
- Ogbuiyi, S. (2015). Use of library and Information Resources: Library Use Education. Lagos, Emaphine Publishers. 1(1): 25-34.
- Ohadinma D. C. , Uwaoma N. 2000 Industrial personnel management Rescue Publishers Owerri, Nigeria
- Ononogbo R. U. 2008 Architect's brief for the design and construction of a university library building: A model draft

Communicate: Journal of Library and Information Science 10 (1) 67 - 77

- P. R. Wadje, Total Quality Management, Journal of Textile Association, Jan.- Feb.,2006,pp 207-213.
- PIERCE, WILLIAM (S). Furnishing the library interior. New York: Marcel Dekker, 1980.
- Powell, T C. Total quality management as competitive advantage: A review and empirical Study. Strategic Management Journal, 16, 1995, pp. 15-37.
- Powell, T. C. (1995). Total quality management as competitive advantage: a review and empirical study. Strategic management journal, 16(1), 15-37.
- Pugh D.S. , Hickson D.J. 2007 Great writers on organisations: The third omnibus edition 3rd rev. ed. Ashgate Publishing Farnham, United Kingdom
- R. D. Stueart and B. B. Moran, "Library and Information Center Management", 7th Ed. Libraries Unlimited, Westport, 2007
- Raney, C. (1988). Time management in the elementary school media center. North Carolina Libraries, 46(1), 18-21.
- Ranganathan, S.R. Library Manual for Library Authorities, Librarians and Library Workers. New Delhi: UBS, 1988. Print. Library Administration. Bangalore: Sarada Ranganathan Endowment for Library Science, 1959. Print.
- Rao, Y Venkata & Sinha M K (2003). Managing Professionals for Successful IT Application in Libraries. In www.johnstark.com, Searched on 17.08.2007.
- Rodrigues C. A. 2001 Fayol's 14 principles of management then and now: A framework for managing today's organisations effectively Management Decision 39 (10) 880 - 889 DOI : 10.1108/EUM0000000006527
- Ross, J. Total Quality Management: Text, cases and readings. Delray Beach, FL.: St. Lucie.1995.
- S. N. Umeozor ,International Journal of Knowledge Content Development & Technology Vol.8, No.3, 29-40 (September, 2018)
- S.K.Pandey,Management of preserving resource in digital library in Indian scenario, University
- Samuelson, H. (1981). Increasing public library productivity. Library Journal, 106(3), 309-311.

- Schein E. H. 1984 Coming to a new awareness of organisational culture Sloan Management Reviews (Winter) 3 - 16
- Scientific Data As a New Component of Library Servicewww.igroup.com.cn/doc/D1- 5_QingLi-Demo%20Version_ENG.pdf
- Senge P. 1990 The fifth discipline Doubleday New York
- Shahaji S. Waghmode, Role INFLIBNET in Growth and Development of higher education, University News,52 (06)February 10-16,2014 11-13.
- Sinclair, D., & Zairi, M. Benchmarking best-pr ctice performance measurement within companies using total quality management. Benchmarking for Quality Management & Technology, 2, (3), 1995, pp.53-71.
- SRIDHAR(M S). "Ratio analysis technique: a tool for assessing the health of a library". In: Financial Management of Library and Information Centers : Papers Presented in XII IASLIC National Seminar at Banaras Hindu University, Varanasi, 28-31 December1986. Calcutta; IASLiC, 1986, p. 137-146.
- Stroh L. K., Northcraft G. B., Neale M. A. 2002 Organisational behavior: A management challenge Lawrence Erlbaum Mahwah, NJ
- Susan Healy, "ISO 15489 Records Management- its Development and Significance". Records Management Journal. 11.3 (2001):133-142. Print.
- Taylor F. W. 1911 The principles of scientific management Harper & Row New York
- Tejomurty, A. (1987). Studies in Academic Librarianship. Jaipur: Printwell.' Tripathi, P. C. and Reddy, P. N. (1991). Principles of Management, 2nd ed. New Delhi: Tata McGraw Hill.
- Total Quality Management by, Devanand Uttam, Department of Mechanical Engineering of G.Z.S. College of Engineering & Technology, Bathinda pg.417-421..
- Understanding Total Quality Management in Contest: Qualitative Research on Managers; Awareness of TQM Aspects in the Greek Service Industry by Alexandros G. Psychologios, The Qualitative Report Volume 12 Number 1 March 2007, pg 40- 66.
- University Computing Center. Records Management: Best

Practice Guidelines; Part 2 Fundamentals of Information and Records Management. Web.11 may 2013. <http://ocla.ucc.ie/records/rm_gpt02.html#21>.

- University News,49(45)November 07-13,2011, 1-7.
- V. S. P. Rao, "Human Resource Management: Text and Cases", 2nd Ed, New Delhi: Excel Books, 2005
- V. Vroom, "Work and Motivation", 3rd Ed. New York: Wiley, 2000.
- van Deusen, J. D. (1996). An analysis of the time use of elementary school library media specialists and factors that influence it. School Library Media Quarterly, 24(2), 85-92.
- Walster, D. (1993). Managing time: A how-to-do-it manual for librarians. New York: Neal-Schuman Publishers, Inc.
- Winston, M. D., & Hoffman, T. (2005). Project Management in Libraries. Journal of Library Administration, 42(1), 51–61. doi:10.1300/j111v42n01_03
- Witzel M. 2003 Fifty key figures in management Routledge London
- Wren D. A., Bedeian A. G., Breeze J. D. 2002 The foundations of Henri Fayol's administrative theory Management Decision 40 (9) 906 - 918 DOI : 10.1108/00251740210441108
- Y. Hamidi, "The effect of performance appraisal result on personnel's motivation and job promotion." Australian Journal of Basic and Applied Sciences, vol. 4, no. 9, pp. 4178-4183, 2010.